"I am delighted to hear of the publication of Dr. Kenneth Ulmer's new book, *Passing the Generation Blessing*. The theme addresses an essential value that every family should embrace, and the author is a leader who has modeled this message in his ministry, marriage, and home. Ken is a personal friend, in whom I can fully attest to the depth of his character, strength of his ministry, verification of his ability, and the fruitful impact of his ministry in Los Angeles, across the United States, and in nations of the world where he has ministered."

**Jack Hayford**
Chancellor emeritus, The King's University

"In this insightful work, my good friend Dr. Kenneth Ulmer challenges, encourages, and convicts us about the absolute necessity of providing a spiritual legacy for the next generation. *Passing the Generation Blessing* will equip God's people to fight and win the battle for ourselves and for those who are looking to us to victoriously guide them into the future of God's blessing."

**Dr. Tony Evans**
President, The Urban Alternative
Senior pastor, Oak Cliff Bible Fellowship

"From the many books written by Dr. Kenneth Ulmer, a prolific speaker, author, and scholar, I find none more compelling or important to the believer than this new release, *Passing the Generation Blessing*. With more than fifty years of ministry experience, one of my greatest heartbreaks is to see how few leaders pass a legacy to the next generation. Pastors rarely prepare for their successor, dads fail to bless their children, church leaders build ministries without making disciples, and the next generation waits for someone to pass them the baton . . . but they wait in vain. This book will ignite a new passion that will drive you to biblical, Spirit-filled action. Bless and empower the next generation before it's too late."

Pres

D0855149

"I have been great friends with Ken for many years, and I believe God has uniquely gifted him to make the Bible relevant in every area of our lives. In his new book, *Passing the Generation Blessing*, he explains how important it is for us to share the stories about God's work in our lives, because our testimonies can change lives. If you want to have an impact on the next generation, you have to tell your story!"

**Robert Morris**

Lead senior pastor, Gateway Church
Bestselling author of *The Blessed Life*,
*The God I Never Knew*, and *Frequency*

"For the better part of my life I have had a front-row seat to view the faithfulness of God as both told and modeled by the life and ministry of my godfather, Bishop Kenneth Ulmer. What he writes in this book, he has done for me—passed the baton. Bishop Ulmer is not entering the winter years of his life as some curmudgeon, but as a godly patriarch who is leveraging the odometer of his life to invest in the coming generations for a time he will not see. Reading *Passing the Generation Blessing*, you will be inspired to tell your story!"

**Bryan Loritts**

Senior pastor, Abundant Life Christian Fellowship,
Mountain View, CA
Author of *Insider/Outsider*

"Challenging. Provoking. Encouraging. Biblical. Hopeful. Wow! These are some of my first responses to *Passing the Generation Blessing* by my friend Bishop Kenneth Ulmer. His ability to translate ancient biblical texts into twenty-first-century parlance is unparalleled. However, what I love most about this book is that the messenger is the message. Bishop Ulmer's internal personal congruence is personified in this book. You'll learn, grow, and share this with all Christian leaders you know—I did."

**Sam Chand**

Leadership consultant and author of *Leadership Pain*

"Kenneth Ulmer takes you through a transformative path to partner with the next generation by passing on a godly legacy. He is a prolific writer, leader, pastor, and brother in Christ. Our partnership stems from our history with Empowered21, a network of global ministries addressing the challenges of the Spirit-empowered church in the twenty-first century. *Passing the Generation Blessing* is a much-needed resource that will benefit both parents and children. The practical stories and history that flow forth from this book will enrich your life far beyond the time you spend reading them and will help you further engrain many of life's lessons God shares with us in His Word."

**Ossie Mills**
Vice president of communications and marketing,
Oral Roberts University
Executive director, Empowered21

"This generation is longing to be fathered, mentored, and nurtured by those who have walked under a grace and favor that must be released so that generations to come will fulfill the call on their lives. *Passing the Generation Blessing* is a seminal work that must be read by all who lead in this milieu."

**Jody Moore**
Senior pastor, Praise Tabernacle Bible Church, Chino, California

"Often times as followers of Christ, many of us lose our way. We lose our identity. We lose our purpose. In his new book, *Passing the Generation Blessing*, my dear brother Bishop Ken Ulmer points us to the way back and the way up by clearly illuminating our path to be blessed and to be a blessing. Today the world is ever so lost and broken. What is to come for the next generation? We are all called to the way of truth and righteousness by passing on the generation blessing. Thank you, Bishop Ulmer, for writing this powerful and anointed treatise, and may God be glorified in all we do."

**Frank Sontag**
Founder, KMG Ministries

"Why do organizations and nations gradually decline over time? Why is it that the first generation generates; the second generation motivates; the third generation speculates; and the fourth generation dissipates? The answer is found in how the leader passes the baton of blessing to the next generation. In *Passing the Generation Blessing*, Dr. Kenneth Ulmer clearly explains how to pass the leadership blessing to the generations that follow for multipliable and maximized success! Dr. Ulmer teaches us how to prepare, plan, and process for 'generational wins!'"

**Dr. James O. Davis**
Founder and president, Cutting Edge International
Global Church Network, Orlando, Florida

"An inheritance is lost and succession broken when the impartation of those who have journeyed well is not carefully bestowed upon capable sons and daughters. Equally as distressing is the reality of successors who dismiss the lasting value in the wisdom and blessing of well-seasoned leaders. Dr. Kenneth C. Ulmer, in *Passing the Generation Blessing*, builds a masterful case for intergenerational continuity and revives the mandate for us to not only 'run well' but to 'finish well.'"

**Wayne Chaney Jr.**
Senior pastor, Antioch Church of Long Beach

"I can think of no one better to communicate the importance of this generational 'passing on' than Bishop Ken Ulmer. Filled with biblical depth and practical guidance for those who are at the season of imparting and for the coming generation who won't be all they can be without that impartation, *Passing the Generation Blessing* is a must-read."

**Steve Riggle**
Founding pastor, Grace Church (grace.tv)

SPEAK LIFE,
SHAPE DESTINIES

# PASSING THE GENERATION BLESSING

## KENNETH C. ULMER, PH.D.

WORTHY®
PUBLISHING

Copyright © 2018 by Kenneth C. Ulmer
Published by Worthy Books, an imprint of Worthy Publishing Group, a division of Worthy Media,
Inc., One Franklin Park, 6100 Tower Circle, Suite 210, Franklin, TN 37067.
WORTHY is a registered trademark of Worthy Media, Inc.

HELPING PEOPLE EXPERIENCE THE HEART OF GOD

eBook available wherever digital books are sold.

Cataloging-in-Publication Data is on file with the Library of Congress.

All rights reserved. No portion of this book may be reproduced, stored in a retrieval system, or trans-
mitted in any form or by any means—electronic, mechanical, photocopy, recording, scanning, or
other—except for brief quotations in critical reviews or articles, without the prior written permission
of the publisher.

Scripture quotations marked KJV are taken from the King James Version of the Bible. Public do-
main. | Scripture quotations marked NIV are taken from the Holy Bible, New International Version®,
NIV®. Copyright © 1973, 1978, 1984, 2011 by Biblica, Inc.™ Used by permission of Zondervan.
All rights reserved worldwide. www.zondervan.com. The "NIV" and "New International Version" are
trademarks registered in the United States Patent and Trademark Office by Biblica, Inc.™ | Scripture
quotations marked CEV are from the Contemporary English Version. Copyright © 1991, 1992, 1995
by American Bible Society. Used by Permission. | Scripture quotations marked ESV are taken from the
ESV® Bible (The Holy Bible, English Standard Version®), copyright © 2001 by Crossway, a publish-
ing ministry of Good News Publishers. Used by permission. All rights reserved. | Scripture quotations
marked NKJV are taken from the New King James Version®. Copyright © 1982 by Thomas Nelson.
Used by permission. All rights reserved. | Scripture quotations marked NLT are taken from the *Holy
Bible*, New Living Translation, copyright © 1996, 2004, 2015 by Tyndale House Foundation. Used
by permission of Tyndale House Publishers, Inc., Carol Stream, Illinois 60188. All rights reserved. |
Scripture quotations marked MSG are taken from *THE MESSAGE*, copyright © 1993, 1994, 1995,
1996, 2000, 2001, 2002 by Eugene H. Peterson. Used by permission of NavPress. All rights reserved.
Represented by Tyndale House Publishers, Inc. | Scripture quotations marked ISV are taken from the
Holy Bible: International Standard Version. Release 2.0, Build 2015.02.09. Copyright © 1995–2014
by ISV Foundation. ALL RIGHTS RESERVED INTERNATIONALLY. Used by permission of
Davidson Press, LLC. | Scripture quotations marked TLB are taken from The Living Bible copy-
right © 1971 by Tyndale House Foundation. Used by permission of Tyndale House Publishers Inc.,
Carol Stream, Illinois 60188. All rights reserved. The Living Bible, TLB, and the The Living Bible
logo are registered trademarks of Tyndale House Publishers. | Scripture quotations marked GNT are
from the Good News Translation in Today's English Version—Second Edition. Copyright © 1992 by
American Bible Society. Used by Permission.

For foreign and subsidiary rights, contact rights@worthypublishing.com

Published in association with Ted Squires Agency, Nashville, Tennessee

ISBN: 978-1-68397-248-8

Cover designed by Kent Jensen | Knail
Interior design and typesetting by Bart Dawson

*Printed in the United States of America*
18 19 20 21 22  BP  8 7 6 5 4 3 2 1

We journey through life as links in a divine chain. Our lives are synthesized with the lives of gifts from God. We press toward the mark with partners of prayer who inspire us to look beyond ourselves and reach into the future. I honor a few of those from whom I have received blessings and through whom I have released blessings.

*To my partner in life, Togetta* . . . For over four decades, you have been and forever shall be the apple of my eye, the beat of my heart, the wind beneath my wings. Christ has been my Savior. You have been my sweetheart.

*To my partners in ministry, Len Sweet and James Davis* . . . You have inspired, encouraged, and enriched my life. We have traveled the globe together, bridging generations for the kingdom.

*To my partner on the podium, Barbara Allen* . . . God granted us the honor of leading His people into His presence. You have been a gift to my life.

*To my parent in the Spirit, Larry Titus* . . . I am constantly amazed at how you juggle those of us who call you father, and treat us as an only child.

*To Dr. Melvin Wade* . . . I am honored to have come forth from your spiritual loins. You passed the baton of scholastic and theological excellence, and blessed me with a hunger and thirst for the Word of God.

*To The Men of Macedonia: Jody Moore, Demetrius Miles, Wayne Chaney, De'Andre Salter, and Van Moody* . . . I am constantly humbled and honored to call you sons. You are gifts to my life. I pass the baton of global influence to you. Steward it well—and pass it on.

*To my son in the Spirit, LL Cool J* . . . We have come a long way from that hospital room in New York. We have seen the best of times and the worst of times. I have been honored to see the hand of God over your life. You are my beloved son.

# CONTENTS

*Foreword by LL Cool J*                                        *xi*

*Introduction by M. Rutledge McCall*                           *xv*


1. Tell Your Story                                              1

2. Pass the Baton                                              17

3. Talk God Talk                                               35

4. Toss Your Mantle                                            49

5. Learn to Listen                                             67

6. Pray for Them                                               85

7. Fight for Them                                              97

8. Go to War                                                  115

9. Take Them to the Mountain                                  143

10. Take the Stage                                            157

11. Know Your Limitations                                     183

12. Tell God's Story                                          207


*Acknowledgments*                                            *229*

*Notes*                                                      *232*

# FOREWORD

The first thing that went through my mind when Bishop Ulmer asked me to write this is that I'm too young to be writing a foreword in a book about passing the baton to the next generation. Then I realized maybe that is just ego, maybe that's just a part of me that wants to hold on to yesteryear, a part of me that I should let go of so that I can grab hold of all the new potential inside of me. Embracing the ideas in this book requires unselfishness and a willingness to prepare yourself so you can help others prepare.

This book is about the seasons when your life was damaged. And about the actions that were taken to repair those damages, to make it to the next season, and to pay the lessons forward so the next generation wouldn't have to experience the trials and tribulations that you did.

I'm a grandfather. Some might say a young grandfather, but that is beside the point. There are younger generations within and outside of my lineage that deserve to benefit from the lessons

I've learned. And the lessons that all of us experienced folks have learned. Bishop Ulmer has helped guide my life. He has imparted and shared wisdom with me for years—Sunday through Monday. I've learned to put aside my ego, I've learned to drop the façade and ask for help, and this book is definitely going to be even more helpful.

Ask yourself this question: Are you willing to step aside and take a back seat in order to bless the younger generations with the wisdom, insight, and experience you've gained? Or are you going to hold on to that experience because of fear and deny yourself entry into your next level of greatness? Look at passing the generation blessing as if it were an already lit candle, and you have the opportunity to share its flame with as many brand-new unlit candles as possible. A lit candle maintains its flame, losing nothing but creating more light, when we light the other candles around us. That's what love does. It gives, it shares, it creates more light.

That's what God said: Let there be light. So the principles in this book, the stories in this book, are a challenge to you and me. Though it may remind us of some of the foolish things we have done, this book will also inspire us and future generations to make wise decisions moving forward. It will embolden us to live out our own personal stories to the fullest. Can you handle that idea? Or are you going to let the past hold your future hostage?

Future generations need us, and we need them. Future generations should inform our decisions today, because what we do today informs the future generations. So embrace the wisdom, ideas, and concepts in this book. They say fool me once shame on you, fool me twice shame on me—but what if you are just fooling yourself? Here's a one-word answer: Don't! This book will help you see the truth.

My grandmother used to say if a task is once begun, never leave it till it's done, be thy labor great or small, do it well or not at all. I suggest you do it well. Read, absorb, and enjoy *passing the generation blessing.*

—LL COOL J

*Actor, rapper, two-time GRAMMY Award winner,*
*Kennedy Center Honoree*

# INTRODUCTION

In my former capacity as managing senior editor of one of the publishers honored to have distributed a number of Dr. Kenneth Ulmer's books, as a developmental editor of Christian living and theology books by noted authors and pastors around the world, as a former literary career senior executive, and as an author myself, I am always thrilled when Dr. Ulmer publishes a new book. And this particular book, a teaching of the urgency of passing this generation's blessings, lessons, and accumulated wisdom and experiences to the next generation, is one of the most crucial and timely works of the new millennium—particularly in light of the state of affairs of this present generation.

On a personal note, I have been blessed and humbled to know Dr. Ulmer for going on fifteen years. I have attended many of his church services, heard scores of his sermons, and read all of his books. Simply put, he is like no other teacher/preacher I have learned from. He is in a rarified echelon of leaders, professors, pastors, and teachers who truly *gets it*. He not only has the heart of the Lord, but he is uniquely gifted at "unpacking," disseminating, and explaining the Word of God like precious few of his national and international peers. And now, with *Passing the Generation Blessings* , he has done it again.

Bishop Ulmer has a style and approach to teaching Scripture that imbues the Word with vibrancy and a revelation of the heart and purpose of God. And he does it in such a way that the reader is not only transfixed and illuminated but is filled with a fresh understanding of the Bible. He can go deep yet make it so instantly understandable that you don't have to come up for air. He can keep it light, yet you feel it right into the marrow of your bones. He can zero in on Scripture like a laser beam, creating those internal *Ahh—now I get it!* moments. He can bring an unnatural hush over a congregation. He can get them to their feet, shouting for joy or crying out to God for mercy.

Dr. Ulmer doesn't merely possess a gift; he is one. He's a man who doesn't merely teach the Word of God—he lives it. And he has fun doing both! If anyone is a generational example, a man to emulate, it is Pastor Kenneth C. Ulmer. I am woefully unworthy of calling this amazing man my friend. Yet, he is. And always will be.

—M. Rutledge McCall
*Author and ghostwriter of books, film, and TV*

## CHAPTER 1

# TELL
# YOUR STORY

*Since my youth, God, you have taught me,*
*and to this day I declare your marvelous deeds.*
*Even when I am old and gray, do not forsake me, my God,*
*till I declare your power to the next generation,*
*your mighty acts to all who are to come.*

PSALM 71:17–18 NIV

Everyone on earth has a story to tell. Whether you realize it or not, your story is an instrument by which you speak to the next generation. If you want to have a positive impact on a future generation, all you have to do is *tell your story.*

Psalm 71 is not attributed to a specific biblical author, but since it is connected to Psalm 70 (which is clearly designated as one of the Davidic psalms), it is believed that Psalm 71 was also written by David. In this psalm, King David prayed a plea to God for an opportunity to speak to the next generation so that he may declare God's power to them, thereby giving them a testimony of the Creator of the universe. David had been walking with the Lord for a long time when he penned this psalm, and as he walked, his story developed.

In beseeching God for the opportunity to speak and to declare His might to the next generation in Psalm 71, David is essentially saying, "Man, have I got an amazing story to tell!" That would actually be one of the understatements of history, because David's riveting testimony is a crucial part of the story of modern Israel.

In David's prayer for a transgenerational ministry through the story about the marvelous deeds he witnessed God perform throughout his life so far, three elements are highlighted: *timing*, *teaching*, and *testimony*.

## THE TIMING OF THE TEXT

David speaks during the season of his life when he is older. We can't be sure about his exact age, but he's in the twilight season of his life. He's an old man. More mature. He's not a shepherd boy anymore. He's not the little kid going after the bear. No longer the boy who took on the lion. Not the teenager with the five smooth stones and the slingshot who took out Goliath. He's now a seasoned, elderly saint. Yet he sees and prays for more years and for more time. *Lord, give me another shot!*

One of the most magnificent stage dramas I have ever seen is Lin-Manuel Miranda's production of *Hamilton*. This award-winning show about the times and tensions of the birth of America is uniquely presented in the rap genre. Many thought it would flop. However, it has proven to be one of the most successful Broadway productions ever. One of the signature songs in the musical features Alexander Hamilton and the cast declaring their refusal to miss the historical opportunity at freedom and the formation of a new country. Hamilton declares he has a shot at changing the world, a shot at changing life in the new land. With amazing musical virtuosity, he and the cast refuse to lose the chance to make history. He will take his shot.

> *We're gonna rise up! Time to take a shot!*
> *We're gonna rise up! Time to take a shot!*[1]

David was a psalmist, but I'm pretty sure he wasn't a rapper. Yet, here in his prayer, he says, *Lord, I still have time to take a shot!* A shot at the next generation. A shot at up-and-coming kingdom leaders. Lord, give me another shot!

I am writing this book after recently celebrating my seventieth birthday. I don't know if David was older or younger than me when he penned Psalm 71, but both he and I would qualify for the "senior saints" category. When my wife and I were at dinner, celebrating my birthday, I said to her, "Wow! Seventy! That's a lot of years." And she said, "Seventy is just a number." Yeah . . . a BIG number! I'm sure I'm in the ballpark of David. David speaks this prayer from the interesting perspective of three points of view:

1. He looks back at *where he was*—that is, turf upon which he has already trodden.
2. He looks around to *where he is*, in the here and now.
3. He looks forward to *where he is going*, wherever God may take him in the future.

By these three perspectives, David is taking us on a journey, a brief synopsis, of his life. He begins with his own birth. "From birth, I have relied on you," he says. "You brought me forth from my mother's womb. I will ever praise you" (v. 6 NIV). *God, from birth You have had Your hand on me.* One version says, "You are he who took me from my mother's womb" (ESV), which is akin to the process of a midwife delivering a child. David paints a picture of his birth as though God Himself were the one actually delivering him from his mother's womb. The implication is that David is alive and has survived all he has because God has had His hand on David all the days of his life.

In the culture of that time, premature births and deaths at birth were not at all unusual. Sometimes the mother died at the birth of her baby. And sometimes both mother and child perished in the process. Because deaths at birth were not unusual, David doesn't take his own birth lightly or for granted. He says to God, "You were there. You had Your hand on me since I came from my mother's womb." In other words, *I'm not here by accident.* This is a key concept. God had His hand on David from the very beginning of his life, from when God brought him forth from his mother's womb.

My generation (which, in colloquial terms, is called the "baby boomers") is like no generation before in the history of the world. It has set a high mark for abortions.[2] Countless lives didn't make it through the womb and on to viable, sentient vibrancy during this generation. We will never know how many of those lives might have made it to maturation had their parents only been told about, grasped, and accepted testimony about a Savior who could bring them through any challenge had they only been told His story. Alas, the boomer generation, which has more abilities and modes and mediums and platforms to tell and to hear stories than any generation in history—the best stories, the most powerful and impactful lessons, stories with the power to change entire lives—isn't being told as they could be and *should* be told about the power of God to impact individual lives as well as entire generations.

A preacher friend of mine, whom God has used in a unique way to bless countless people, has an incredible story. When his mother was carrying him in her womb, she tried to abort him. But the abortion failed. So, she tried a second time. And that attempt was also unsuccessful. Her son is now a preacher of the gospel, and souls are being saved through him. His testimony, like David's, shows how God had His hand on his life. This man didn't have to be here on earth. He could have gone from the womb straight to heaven. But God had a plan and a purpose for his life. A killing was planned. A killing was thwarted, once. Thwarted again. Then, a life—a bountiful, vibrant, powerful life—came forth from that which was intended for death. And that man's life ushered countless people from another type of death—a spiritual, God-less living death—and into the best kind of life. Now *that's* a story! *I was marked for death, but God said, "You shall not die; you shall live to tell your story!"*

Wow!

King David had a story too. His powerful testimony is that he *made it all the way*. He might not have made it, but God had His hand on David from when he was a strapping young kid, all the way through a powerful living testimony of his life, and right into a ripe old age. Just like God had His hand on my preacher friend. And David lived and grew and learned and experienced and accomplished and prospered. He made it.

Likewise, your testimony is that you didn't have to be here. But you are. Which means that your testimony goes all the way back to your birth, because you're not here by accident: you are on earth by divine design, placed here by a graceful God *for a purpose.*

David says, "From my birth, You have had Your hand on me, God." Then he says, "From my youth, my confidence has been in You." *Youth.* The teenage years. The crazy season. Years when nobody could tell you anything, because you knew everything. You knew it all. You were *tha bomb*, king of the hill, author of your own life, and the world was your oyster. And you made certain choices, many of which you later may have wished you had never made, because one day in your future you finally came to understand that those choices didn't represent who you really wanted to be. The legacy you had been weaving and the examples you had been setting for the next generation were not what you wanted to represent. And what got you through it all was exactly what got David through his crazy season too: God's grace alone.

David says, "From my youth"—my teenage years—"God has had His hand on me." He says, "In my youth I learned that You were my hope." Here's an interesting thought: the Hebrew word for *hope* is the same word for *rope*. David's testimony is that in his crazy years, he learned that God was his rope. Not so much that God was the rope and David held on to Him, but that God was the rope that *held on to David*.

Have you ever let go of the rope? Have you ever been so crazy or lost hope to the point that you tried to cut your own rope? David said when he was crazy enough to turn from God or let God go, he discovered that he could only go so far, because his life was wrapped up, tied up, tangled up, and tethered to God because of His rope of love. What assurance!

What has God's rope yanked you out of? He has yanked me out of nightclubs, out of the wrong building, out of the wrong place at the wrong time, out of the wrong relationship, and on and on. When was the last time you thanked God for His "rope-yanking" ministry in your life? We've all been there. Take a moment and think about where you would be if He hadn't tugged you out of who knows where you shouldn't have been, whether you were there accidentally or deliberately. What if He had not yanked you out of the last place you were in that could have caused some serious problems in your life? What if He had not dragged you out of the last relationship you were in? Where would you have been had it not been for the Lord on your side? Thank God for the rope of hope that saves our crazy selves! To paraphrase Psalm 71:17, David is saying, "Lord, when I was crazy in my youth, You held on to me." God already knew that, of course, but David has come to the realization that God is his rope, his tether, and he is now processing it through the psalm as he prays, "Lord, You held on to me even when I tried to let go of You in those crazy times of my youth. You loved me enough not to let go of me." David's testimony is based on knowing that from his youth, once he claimed God as his Lord and Master, God latched on to him and refused to let go. As David looks at where he is in his life at the time he writes Psalm 71, he tells God what he has learned, what "you have taught me, [Lord]" (v. 17 NIV).

Some versions begin the following verse 18 with the word *now*. Look at how one Bible version translates this verse: "And now that I am old and gray, don't forsake me" (TLB). David had just finished saying in verse 7: "My success—at which so many stand amazed—is because you are my mighty protector" (TLB). It's as if David is saying, "Now I am as a wonder. I was a little baby. I was a crazy teenager. But now I'm a wonder. Now they marvel at me. Now I'm a miracle." He says this because God is his protector. He says that when people look at him now and see his success, all the player-haters stand amazed at how far he has come. "They tried to count me out a long time ago," David declares. "They didn't realize God had His hand on me. My ordinary life became *extra*ordinary because of the *extra* in God's power." David is saying, *I'm a miracle thanks to God's holding power.*

You may not realize it, but there's a miracle in your home, at your workplace, in your church pews. You're a miracle because God kept His hand on you. When people look at you, if they can't understand the success you have, it's because they don't realize what a miraculous story you have to tell.

According to *Merriam Webster's Collegiate Dictionary*, the word *miracle* means "an extraordinary event manifesting divine intervention in human affairs." When the devil tells you that you will never make it, tell him you're a miracle. God has done something in your life that no one can explain in the natural. If you've ever gone back home to visit and come across folks who thought you would never amount to anything or said you wouldn't do something significant with your life, you need to learn to look at them and say, "Well, look at me now"—not to brag about who you are, but to point out the fact that He who lives within you is greater than he who is out to get you.

You have those "nobody but God" spots in your life that amount to a powerful testimony and a miraculous story to tell the next generation. We all have some "nobody but God" stories. All we need to do is deliberately recall them. You have some seasons in your life that you can point back to and say, "God alone did that."

When God blesses you, He doesn't do it in secret. He prepares a table before you. He sends out an invitation to all the haters who said you would never be there. And when they see your success, they can't explain it. So just tell them, "Nobody but God." Declare God's marvelous deeds in your life. Tell your story—and give God the glory in the story. People will not merely look at you differently; they'll look at God in a whole new light. They'll want some of whatever He did for you.

## THE TEACHING IN THE TEXT

When David says, "O God, you have taught me" (v. 17 NLT), the timing is a crossroad in his life when he is looking back at the *already* while standing in the *now* and poised on the threshold of the *yet to come*, and he remembers: *God has taught me!*

There are several implications suggested in the word *taught*. The form of the word here means "to cause to learn." This means if you had not been taught, you could not have learned. For example, even when I have taught someone through my lectures or sermons or talks, I never assume that the person actually learned what I intended them to learn. All I can confidently assume is that I did the teaching. But the *learning* part of the equation does not take place without the *active involvement of the learner.* It's a two-way street.

David learned. He says, "You have taught me," which means, *I've learned some things in my life.*

Interestingly, the word for *teach* is also the word used for the phrase to *teach warfare*. It is the same word that is used to teach soldiers how to go to battle. David is essentially saying that God taught him as he was maturing, and specifically taught him how to do battle with the enemy. David says, "I have learned how to fight him." *I have learned how to go to war.*

When I was growing up in East St. Louis, Illinois, at Mount Zion Missionary Baptist Church, the people of God would often sing songs like "I'm a Soldier in the Army of the Lord" or

PASSING THE GENERATION BLESSING

"I Am on the Battlefield for My Lord." One of the popular songs in the Christian hymnody was "Onward, Christian Soldiers," marching as to war. What's interesting about saints who sing about being Christian soldiers in the army of the Lord on the battlefield for God is that so many saints freak out when they get shot at! Here's a news flash: it is the job description of the enemy to shoot at us Christians! By taking potshots at us, the enemy is merely doing what the enemy does: he tries to get us out of the battle, to sideline us, wound us, make us casualties of war, render us useless in the plan of God. In fact, his goal really isn't merely to wound or hurt you. He wants to take you out! He comes to kill, steal, and destroy (John 10:10).

Here's a third dimension of being taught: *experience.* The verb form used means *to cause to learn, teach to war,* and *to experience.* This means that when you say, "Lord, You have taught me something," you are actually saying, *God, You have allowed me to experience something.*

God always has a reason for teaching us. For example, teaching is driven by a purpose or an intention, such as wanting someone to learn a particular lesson. Or teaching might not be specifically intended, such as when one is taught by an experience or observation (which essentially becomes the "teacher" of the lesson). The constant is that there is an action—the *teaching*—followed by a quid pro quo reaction, the *learning.* In other words, when God has *taught* you about His love, it means you have *experienced* His love, you have learned about His love (whether or not you are aware of it or acknowledge it).

The fact that God does not teach without a specific purpose in mind means that your walk with God is never merely theoretical; it is also practical and with intent. It's not merely about what you believe; it's also about how you behave. This is an experiential lesson, which is followed by the acquisition of the learning, which is followed by the application of the lesson. Thus, the progression is: *God taught me. I learned. I applied. God's purpose is fulfilled.*

## THE TESTIMONY IN THE TEXT

Here's the key to the whole message: when David says, "I will declare" (v. 15 ISV), he is saying, *I will give forth a testimony*. To "give forth" means *to tell about, to announce, to reveal*. The importance of giving forth our testimony, of telling others about our experience of God, is in the fact that He wants to *use* our declaration of testimony. One way God uses our testimony is to overcome the enemy. The enemy is described in Revelation 12:9 as "that ancient serpent called the devil, or Satan" (NIV). Our declaration of testimony, as revealed in Revelation 12:11, is that we overcome the enemy by the word of our testimony.

Contrary to present time, previous generations knew nothing about things like internet dating websites and instant access to all manner of sexual debauchery and about "sexting" images via so-called "smart" phones. So, how do we overcome the devil when he seems to be throwing more at us than at any previous generation? How do we stand against an enemy who uses attacks the variety and likes of which our own parents never faced? How should you handle all of these distractions and temptations and diversions from the will of God? You do it by making yourself aware of one crucial fact: the devil does not come to merely hurt you, he comes to *steal, kill,* and *destroy* you—utterly and completely. That is his sole mission, his *raison d'être*, his main purpose as he goes to and fro about the earth. *He. Wants. Your. Soul.* Period!

The way you overcome the devil is through the blood of the Lamb and by the active and kinetic word of your testimony. A testimony is "evidence," it is "witness," it is "firsthand authentication of a fact." In other words, speak it out! Your testimony is truth. It is power. You have victory by the words of your testimony.

Sometimes the teacher is God. Sometimes the teacher is circumstances. Sometimes the teacher is our own choices and decisions. However, regardless of the teacher, here is a principle of life: what the teacher teaches, the teacher tests! It is the test that produces your *test*imony! Notice how you can't even spell *testimony* without getting past the *t-e-s-t* part? This means we cannot have the victory until we get past the test.

David had some tests (or, as he phrases it in Psalm 71:20 [NIV], "you have made me see troubles, many and bitter"), yet he learned how to come through them. And when he came through them by passing the test, he had a *test*imony: "I will praise you more and more. My mouth will tell of your righteous deeds, of your saving acts all day long," he writes in Psalm 71:14–15 (NIV).

Too many people today want a testimony without a test. They want a freebie. A pass. An easy way forward. But there is no such thing, not with the devil on the march, breathing down our necks, looking for any weakness in our armor, any distraction to pull us from the battlefield and sink us down into his muck and mire. The only way to get a *test*imony—that is, to gain the ability to authenticate a fact from firsthand experience—is to first get into, get through, and get past the *test*.

If you look carefully at your life and the tests you have taken—*you won!* You're still here. You came through it. You may not have even *known* you were in a test. Has God brought you through a test? If He did bring you through a test, then it resulted in a testimony, which you now have to give. Maybe it was a test that tried to take you out. Or perhaps it was a test that said you have no value in this world. Or a test that convinced you that you could not conquer what had been trying to overcome you. A test that said you will never rise again. A test that you thought would reduce you to nothing. Or that tried to convince you that you would never prosper. Or you'd never succeed. Yet God pulled you out of the mess, and in the middle of the test, He gave you a testimony.

Walk around your house and look at your children, and deliberately recall a time when you didn't know if you would ever even have a child. Walk around your house and look in your closet and see how God clothes you. Go to your garage and look at the car you drive, when maybe you used to take the bus everywhere. Maybe you were once turned down for a job you were fully qualified for, yet God gave you a position that you weren't quite qualified enough for, because your testimony includes His favor—and that's bigger than any old résumé. We all have something to thank God for; we just need to *deliberately choose to recall* what we went through to be where we are now after having earned a testimony from what we endured to get here.

If you will only persevere, He will bring you through each test. If you will refuse to give up, He will give you a testimony, because He will bring you through. And what we need to learn after we make it through is to give God praise for what we learned through the tests He allowed us to go through—the tests that produced our testimony.

The devil knows that every time we give our testimony, we overcome him. So one of the greatest strategies he will use is to shut your mouth on your testimony. He wants you to be quiet as a church mouse, because he knows that you defeat him every time you speak out your testimony and give glory to God. That's why the enemy will do all he can to silence you completely or get your full attention onto him (whether you realize you're doing that or not) or make you afraid to speak out about God. But you have not been given a spirit of fear, but of power, of love, and of a strong mind, as we are assured in 2 Timothy 1:7. So never recoil when the devil attacks. Stand firm and tell your story. Never give up! Never turn back! It ain't over 'til God says it's over! The devil goes about *acting like* a roaring lion, but the true lion—the Lion of Judah—is your Savior, so you have nothing to fear.

If you want to give the devil a shudder in the midst of your battle, give God a sudden shout of praise— out loud! The enemy will flee like the Midianites from before Gideon when he and his three hundred men blew the trumpets and smashed the pots in Judges 7:20–21.

Tell your children God alone gave you your victories. That is how we speak into the next generation. That is how we bless a generation.

You have a story to tell. Fearlessly *tell it*!

# PASS
# THE BATON

*Paul, an apostle of Christ Jesus by the will of God,*
*in keeping with the promise of life that is in Christ Jesus,*
*to Timothy, my dear son: Grace, mercy, and peace from God*
*the Father and Christ Jesus our Lord. I thank God, whom I serve,*
*as my ancestors did, with a clear conscience, as night and day*
*I constantly remember you in my prayers. . . . I am reminded of*
*your sincere faith, which first lived in your grandmother Lois*
*and in your mother Eunice and, I am persuaded, now lives*
*in you also. For this reason I remind you to fan into flame the gift*
*of God, which is in you through the laying on of my hands.*

2 TIMOTHY 1:1–3, 5–6 NIV

Both Paul and the Bible use several different ideas, metaphors, and images to describe the life of a believer. Each picture or metaphor releases a story, an image, a narrative. Our mind grasps messages more through the pictures painted by the text than the words themselves. My friend Dr. Leonard Sweet has coined the term "narraphor" to represent this narrative metaphoric picturing. Dr. Sweet wrote, "Because a narraphor is a story made from metaphor, it narrates with metaphorical meaning. The combining of story and image creates a reality into which the listener enters: a narrative that touches life contextually and layers of meaning that offer depth, breadth, and height."[1]

For example, in 2 Timothy 2:3–4, we are referred to as soldiers in the army of the Lord. In other words, God gives us gear for the battle of good versus evil here on earth. In John 15 we are called the branches and He the vine. This means that, without Him, we can do nothing. Please note carefully what Jesus said. He did *not* say, "Without me you cannot do anything." You and I know people who have no relationship with the Lord, but they are busy doing, making, creating, and seemingly accomplishing much. Jesus says, "Without me you *can* do." However, without Him you can do . . . nothing. The essence, the spiritual value, the long-term analysis is: *nothing*! Without Him we can do nothing!

In 1 Corinthians 9:24 we are called athletes. In Ephesians 6:12, we are wrestlers: "We wrestle not against flesh and blood, but against principalities, against powers" (KJV). We are called runners in Hebrews 12:1, running the race with patience and laying aside those things that hinder us as we press toward the mark, forgetting those things that are behind (that is, we don't get off stride looking at the things that are behind us; we focus on the path before us).

In 2 Timothy 4:7, where Paul writes to his spiritual son Timothy, "I have finished the race" (NIV), there is an implied image of the believer not merely as a runner in a race but a runner in a relay race. This relay is a metaphor of one way to pass blessings from one generation to the next. Paul talks *narraphorically* of speaking to the next generation as a "baton handoff." I got this word *narraphor* from my friend Leonard Sweet. He coined this term as a synthesis of a narrative and a metaphor. He is explaining, by using the terminology of an athletic race (just as he does in Hebrews 12:1), how there is continuity in our relationship with God from one generation to the next, with the two interacting at the intersection of the handoff of the mantle (the baton) from one runner (one generation) to the next.

As I'm writing this section, the world has just witnessed the closing ceremonies of the 2018 Winter Olympics in South Korea. I must say, other than the skiing events and the figure skating, I am not a big fan of winter sports. However, I love the Summer Olympics. I can be found glued to the screen during the various gymnastic events, which are mostly individual athletes competing against their opponents, against world records, and against their own personal best records. But most of all I am a faithful fan of the track events, the foot races. My favorites are the relay events. These matches of speed, strategy, and precision gush adrenaline through my system, even though I am merely an armchair spectator.

In the 2008 Beijing Olympics, the 4x100-meter relay races will no doubt go down as some of the most disappointing events in American sports history. Both the US men's *and* women's 4x100-meter relay teams dropped batons during handoffs that year. On the men's team, the botched handoff between Tyson Gay and Darvis Patton cost the team that race (though the US men's 4x100-meter relay team hung on to win gold in the event).[2] Then, in the women's 4x100-meter relay, Lauryn Williams lost the baton to Torri Edwards, disqualifying the team from the race.

A similar thing had happened in the same 4x100-meter relay races four years earlier, at the 2004 Olympics in Athens. Marion Jones (the 2000 Olympics' sprint champion) had run the second leg of the relay well enough to put the women's team into a solid lead, but she fumbled the handoff to Lauryn Williams (though the US women's 4x400-meter relay team went on to take gold in the 2004 Olympics).[3] In the men's 4x100-meter relay that year, Justin Gatlin and Coby Miller muffed a pass after the second leg, which allowed the Brits to pull off an upset win over the second-place Americans by one one-hundredth of a second (but at least the US men's 4x400-meter relay team also won gold in the 2004 Olympics).

All that training, focus, concentration, and practice, practice, practice . . . for split-second missteps that affected history. Was the problem with the athletes or with the batons? The "stick," as the baton is called, isn't particularly fearsome. It's not slippery, not awkwardly shaped, not tricky to handle. The stick is cylindrical, a smidge over eleven and a half inches long, a tad under five inches in circumference, one and a half inches thick, made of wood or aluminum, and weighs only fifteen ounces.

Not frightening in any way. So, what was the handoff problem?

Running is mostly an individual sport, where the athletes are competing against themselves and a clock, and maybe a previous or desired time. But when a race becomes a team sport with physical interaction and a point of contact between two runners, things suddenly become a bit more complex. As a 2012 *New York Times* story on baton drops stated it, "Runners who spend their entire lives trying to ruin the dreams of their competitors suddenly must share them. Success and blame become a joint venture."[4] The competitors now have to collaborate in a finely tuned, carefully planned exchange of a device that has no more to do with running than the size of the number stitched on their tank tops. Yet, this device can make or break the game, lose the competition, embarrass the runner, ruin reputations, and fail to set a record. Even if the athlete is one of the best on the planet.

Complicating matters is that each runner learns how to pass the baton in a different way. There's the underhand sweep style, where the passer brings the stick up from below and sweeps it into the receiver's palm in perfectly choreographed synchronicity. There's the overhand method, in which the stick is slapped into the receiver's hand from above. There's the push, an awkward move where the passer pushes the stick out in front of them like they're pointing a flashlight and shoves it into the receiving runner's back-stretched hand. In other words, a lot can go wrong in any of the techniques. It's all in the handoff. A perfect handoff can make history. So can a botched one. In Beijing in 2008 and Athens in 2004, as the world watched, both the US men's and women's teams dropped the baton. What happened was a botched pass, a bad handoff, a missed opportunity.

Yet, these tragic faux pas don't have to happen. To pass the baton, all you have to do is make that precise exchange of baton from your hand securely into the hand of the next runner. The baton starts with one person, who passes it to the next person. Out of one hand from behind and forward into the next. Essentially, out of one life and into the next life. But there's that split second in which both runners are holding on to and touching the same thing, the same item, the same *revelation*, the same baton, while still moving ahead in unison on the same "topic." Both are holding the same substance, with the goal of passing that substance on; passing something that is in your life into the life of someone else.

The apostle Paul likens the handing off of "transgenerational" faith (that is, one person's faith passed forward from one generation to the next) to the central "race" of a believer's life. Think of it this way: your story—the *race* you have run and are still running—is your life displayed, and the "baton" is your life deposited. In other words, you are depositing parts of your life into someone else's life, into their hands, to make those parts theirs so they, too, can move them forward into their future. And the baton—the essence, the story, the accumulation of your life's experiences and lessons—is what you intentionally deposit into the next generation in order to help lead them to victory. The baton is the words you speak over their life; it is the wisdom you impart to them, your experiences, including successes and failures, that you share with the next generation for their growth, learning, and edification.

Visualize the handoff like this: in athletic relay running events, there is an exchange lane about twenty meters long where runners in the relay are allowed to initiate their exchange. This "fly zone" or "runway" begins at a little triangle and runs to the edge of a big triangle. It is inside this handoff zone that the opportunity exists for the next runner in the relay to both set themselves up to begin running toward the start line and to take possession of what is now their baton—which cannot be fully exchanged or transferred until both runners are completely inside the large triangle, a space known as the "exchange zone." If either runner is outside of that zone before the handoff is completed, they are disqualified.

In order to reduce the likelihood of a dropped stick, the handoff of the baton requires a natural or acquired physical athletic ability along with hand-eye coordination under duress, which requires *relationship*—hopefully a practiced, fluid, and close relationship—between the runners. Likewise, in life there is an exchange zone between one generation and the next, a limited period of time in which our present generation may pass the baton to the future generation. That is, we have a certain period of time to influence, to impact, to help shape the generation coming up. In that zone, our relationship with them is like the passing of a baton from one generation's runners to the next generation's runners. It requires a synchronized relationship between like-minded people on the same team, running for the same goal: *to move knowledge of God forward.*

As Paul speaks to Timothy, he is teaching the young disciple how impacting a generation is done through relationships. A runner on a generational "team" works in tandem in relationship to the next generational team member as the two intersect at a given point in the race of life. When Paul talks to Timothy, he tells him that he has a faith that he received from both his grandmother, Lois, and his mother, Eunice.

In Acts 16, Timothy's father is revealed to be Greek, with the inference being that he was an unbelieving Gentile and an "absentee" father who was either dead by the time Timothy was saved or who had no impact on his son's walk with the Lord. However, while his father was unsaved, Timothy's grandmother, Lois, and mother, Eunice, were Jewish and were saved; that is, they were what some call "completed" or "Messianic" Jews, having come to Christ in fulfillment of Jewish prophecy regarding the Messiah. Thus, Timothy's mom and grandma experienced the profound continuity of both the Old and New Covenants, resulting in a deep and living "sincere faith," which they had passed on to Timothy, the next generation.

Lois and Eunice's faith was genuine to the point where it penetrated their hearts and wills, their fears, hopes, loves, desires, joys, compassions, and zeal. Such faith had come to characterize Timothy as well. This was not a case of good breeding or eugenics; it was the outgrowth of being raised in a home with two parental figures who honored Jesus and displayed their belief to Timothy. This enabled him to not only see the faith demonstrated by these two women of God, but led to him to also become saved, which in turn led to his life becoming a demonstration of honoring Christ as well—and which in turn became an example for countless generations right up to today and beyond, through the Bible.

In addition to having spiritual mothers, God met Timothy's need for a father through the apostle Paul. Though Timothy's natural father was not in the picture, Paul spiritually adopted him and loved him like he was his natural son. God used Paul to pass the baton to his son Timothy, just as Lois had passed the baton on to her daughter Eunice, and Eunice passed the baton on to her son Timothy. Three consecutive generations of a family of believers who honored Jesus made for one powerful family for God.

Some of us are here because of the prayers of a grandmother, mother, Big Mama, Madea, nana. James 5:16 teaches that the effectual, fervent prayer of a righteous person avails much. This was evident in the life of Timothy, who was a living example of the power of three generations of blessings.

Psalms 68:5 tells us that God is a "father to the fatherless" (NIV). He's not a heavenly Father who is distant or unbothered by our struggles. On the contrary, He draws near the brokenhearted. God is aware and faithful to provide us with the things we need spiritually, materially, emotionally, and relationally.

God ordained a father-son relationship between Paul and Timothy to cultivate Timothy's life and cement Paul's legacy. The word for *legacy* is used in two senses: first, in the sense of a seed; and second, in the sense of a name. Thus, one's legacy has to do with passing on a seed, which is the compact culmination of one's "spiritual DNA," the foundation of one's spiritual life. The passing of the name is the foundation of passing one's identity, one's reputation, one's history, along with the blessing.

This 2 Timothy passage says Paul's faith also came from his forefathers, that Paul had served God with the same faith that his forefathers had served with. However, while Paul was a blessing to Timothy, Paul had a legacy of imperfection, meaning that while he served God as his ancestors did, he also took on some of the past baggage of their character flaws. For example, one of Paul's ancestors was Abraham; Abraham was a liar. Paul had another ancestor named Moses; Moses was a murderer. Paul also had a forefather by the name of David—and there are not enough pages in this book to lay out everything that was off-kilter with King David, but suffice it to say he got himself into some pretty messed-up situations that he could have avoided had he thought them through in advance and used his love for God as his counselor.

The point is, when God chooses to bless us through spiritual relationships, He sometimes does it through people who have often missed the mark. Yet, the passing of the baton can still produce profound future results, as proven in the lives of great patriarchs like Abraham, Moses, and David. This means there is profound hope for each of us, through God.

## THE BATON OF GOD'S MIGHTY ACTS

The process of the transmission of the history of salvation from one generation to another is done by the telling of God's "mighty acts" of deliverance. As David puts it, "Let each generation tell its children of your mighty acts; let them proclaim your power" (Psalm 145:4 NLT). In Scripture, the generational handing down of stories of God's works, mercies, and deliverances is the principal mode used to keep the teachings of the lessons at the forefront and helps encourage each successive generation ever onward as God works His purpose in the lives of believers.

God says that our generation must speak to the next generation about His goodness. This means we have a responsibility, an obligation, a duty, to speak to them about Him. The Hebrew word for *speak* is *shabach*, which means "praise"—to praise God, to declare or shout out His mighty acts. We pass the baton (the spiritual substance of the Lord) by praising Him to each upcoming generation. We have a responsibility to let our worship become a witness, a public praise of worship. As we praise God for who He is, for what He does, and for what He has done, this worship becomes a witness to those gathered around us. They are then encouraged to join us in praising God as their faith is strengthened and they pass their stories forward to the generation after them. It's a beautiful perpetual synchronicity of ever-growing generational spiritual blessings.

When blessings come our way, we must remember to relay, to pass the baton (the symbol of our godly substance) to future generations. In other words, tell the next generation where our blessings came from. Tell them of God's bounty and mercy.

There are five "batons" we are to pass forward. Let's take a look at each. . . .

## THE BATON OF BELIEF

Paul believed in Timothy. He knew Timothy would be successful in ministry, so he charged him to "stir up the gift of God which is in you" (2 Timothy 1:6 NKJV). Paul basically told him, "Son, don't let them despise your youth. God has given you an anointing. So don't back off of your calling just because you're young. God is going to show you some things that others won't see." The apostle was telling Timothy that he understood the young man's value and how God wanted to use him.

Unfortunately, our translation of the phrase "stir up the gift of God" loses the vivid metaphor conjured by the word Paul used in 2 Timothy 1:6: *anazopureo* (a word that is used only here in the New Testament). The main part of the word, *zopureo*, refers to embers of a flame that has subsided. However, putting the *ana* in front of *zopureo* changes the meaning to "kindle anew the flames of the fire." In other words, in contemporary terms, Paul is encouraging Timothy to "fan the flames of your giftedness." Which was a warning to Timothy not to let the fire go out. *Don't let your zeal and your passion stagnate.* He affirmed Timothy in his giftedness while inspiring him to maximize his potential.

*This is no time to become passive, kid. Kick it into high gear!*

## THE BATON OF COURAGE

The next baton we are to hand off to the younger generation is the baton of courage. Paul declared that God has not given us a spirit of fear, but a spirit of courage.

Whenever you run into a situation that has the potential to drum up fear within you or frighten you, or if you find yourself afraid to stand for what you know is right or stand against an injustice, you know that reaction didn't come from God. There's not an ounce of fear in God, nor does He ever suggest we be fearful. Second Timothy 1:7 says, "God has not given us a spirit of fear" (NKJV). James 4:7 adds, "Resist the devil and he will flee from you" (NKJV). And 1 Peter 5:9 says, "Resist him, standing firm in the faith" (NIV).

Passing the baton of courage means teaching the next generation the courage to stand, even if you have to stand by yourself. You may come to a situation where nobody is standing but you. Many of us have done so, and will do so again in the future, but God tells you that you have the power, the anointing, the strength, and the calling to do it. You have the courage not to back down, if you choose to exercise it.

Everybody feels nervous apprehension or anxious reluctance now and then in some situations. That's normal. Nobody *wants* to be attacked or ridiculed. It takes courage to stand alone, and it's okay to be different. In fact, we are *called* to be different from the world. Besides, you have nothing to lose, because many people won't respect you if you buckle to them, and they won't accept you anyway, because you are different and have different values than them. So, stand.

I earned my undergraduate degree at the University of Illinois. One time when I was with my fraternity, we visited the Kansas chapter frat house. The brothers from Kansas had these special shirts made up for the anniversary of the fraternity. But I couldn't wear the sweatshirt, because the message emblazoned on it was far from Christian. I knew that if I put on that particular shirt, my mother would put up a righteous fuss about me wearing it. So I was the only guy in the fraternity who didn't wear the shirt. But God gave me the wherewithal to stand through the laughter and ridicule from the other guys. And I bet that somewhere inside every one of those men who snickered, there was a measure of respect for the message I was putting out there with my stand. I wasn't a sheep. Wasn't one of the crowd. I was different. I stood apart. I didn't cave. I was God's man, not the fraternity's.

## THE BATON OF LOVE

The next baton is love, which also happens to be the key to the resistance of fear; as 1 John 4:18 says: "Perfect love drives out fear" (NIV). God has given us a spirit of love. One of the greatest challenges you will face in your life is to learn how to love people you don't like or with whom you disagree. To learn how to love people who don't like you practically defines the life of Jesus. We cannot display the character of God to others if we do not display love, because God *is* love—the very essence, the living embodiment of love. Take a look at 1 Corinthians 13:4–8 and replace the word "love" with the name Jesus, and you will see what love looks like in the flesh.

Every reflection of God should be out of, and a demonstration of, His love. In fact, we are *commanded* to love one another. Dozens of time we're told, in both the Old and New Testament, to love people: Leviticus 19:18 and 19:34, Deuteronomy 10:19, 1 John 3:11 and 3:23, 1 John 4:7, 2 John 1:5, Jude v. 21, and in many other verses. We must always handle others with love. Even with people who make it difficult to love them. Even people with whom we strongly disagree. Love them. That doesn't mean embrace or agree with anything they do or say; it means to love them as in the 1 Corinthians 13:4–8 definition of love. We should always err on the side of love. Love is the standard of God. And it's our duty and responsibility to uphold His standard before all others.

## THE BATON OF DISCERNMENT

Paul wanted his son Timothy to have a sound mind. By sound mind, Paul meant self-discipline, sound judgment, discernment. He wanted Timothy to have the ability to make the right judgment calls and the discernment to come to wise decisions. Discernment is the exercise of a sane and balanced mind.

Discernment guides our efforts and helps us apply intelligence and purpose to our actions. The baton of discernment speaks of times when, faced with choices, we make the right ones; ones that most honor God, even when that means we have to be different from the rest of the crowd.

While discernment is needed at all times, it is particularly needed in dangerous times. Times when foolish, ill-considered, hasty, fanatical actions have the potential to precipitate dire results (particularly when leadership is not "sensibly minded"). What Paul is telling us is that we must retain a measure of control over our thinking and actions that will allow us to take a balanced, "God's-eye" view of any situation. When everything is coming unglued, this quality of levelheadedness is what will keep us focused calmly on the power and love the Holy Spirit provides us. This makes perseverance in life and ministry possible. As Rudyard Kipling put it in *Rewards and Fairies*, "If you can keep your head when all about you are losing theirs and blaming it on you . . . you'll be a man, my son."[5]

If I could reach out of these pages and pray one prayer over you right now as you are reading these words, it would be that you would grow to have discipline over your life. As a pastor, I'm held responsible to pray that over those who attend my church. I know firsthand what it's like to live an undisciplined life. It's counterproductive, confusing, aggravating, dispiriting, and on and on. My heart's desire for you would be that you don't fall into the same holes I did in my youth, but that you would learn to make the right choices and exercise the wisdom and discernment produced by godly judgment.

## THE BATON OF BLESSING

The final baton we pass on to the next generation is the baton of blessing.

Paul says the gift that came upon Timothy's life came through the laying on of hands. That's not something spooky or weird or strange. It's actually powerful and mighty and energizing. It's the affirmation and the blessing of touch. It's not someone slapping you down with oil or smacking you backward with a palm to the forehead. It is the *transfer of blessing.* It's God blessing someone in order to bless you, and you in turn blessing someone else. Pay the blessing forward. Learn how to bless one another. How to encourage someone else. It's a powerful baton to pass on.

The implication in the text is that Timothy grew up without his father around. One of my closest friends once said to me, "I've never called a man *Father.* I never had a daddy." Not only that, but this is the friend whose mother tried to abort him twice. And today he is a minister of the Gospel of Jesus. This man has one of the kindest and godliest spirits, yet he was marked for death two times before he was even born. He's a man who never had a dad, yet he's one of the best fathers I know. And he's passing the blessing of God's love on to the next generation.

It doesn't always matter where you came from or what your situation was at home when you were growing up. Regardless of what you have faced in your life, God can and will bless you. Not only that, but He wants to bless others through you.

Be a blessing to others and wonders will flow from it into future lives you may never even see, like distant batons passing from one hand to the next and the next until nobody will really know where the blessings all started, apart from the hand of God.

On April 6, 2018, at the end of a *PBS NewsHour* interview of ninety-one-year-old Harry Belafonte about how America needs to change, seventy-six-year-old interviewer Charlayne Hunter-Gault changed the topic slightly and asked Belafonte, "So it may be a moment of passing the baton. Are you ready for that?" And Mr. Belafonte replied, "Yes—we have to be ready for it. What are *you* gonna do with the baton?"[6]

I challenge you to pose that same question to yourself: *What am I going to do with the baton?*

I would like to suggest an answer: *Pass it forward to the next generation!*

## CHAPTER 3

# TALK GOD TALK

*Moreover, in those days I saw men of Judah*
*who had married women from Ashdod, Ammon and Moab.*
*Half of their children spoke the language of Ashdod*
*or the language of one of the other peoples,*
*and did not know how to speak the language of Judah.*

NEHEMIAH 13:23–24 NIV

During the nineteenth century there was a German explorer and naturalist named Alexander von Humboldt, who spent much time exploring Central and South America. During one of his explorations on the Orinoco River in Venezuela, Humboldt came across a tribe called the Carib. He discovered that this tribe had several parrots that spoke fragments of a language that was different from the language of the Carib.

Humboldt asked one of the tribesmen where the parrots had come from, and the tribesman explained that they had been among the spoils of war after the Carib tribe had wiped out the Maypure tribe. "We don't know their language," the tribesman said. "We don't speak Maypure, and they are all dead now." Which meant that since the Maypure people had been annihilated, the language of their tribe had died with them. And that meant their parrots were the last on earth to speak it.

These birds were, in fact, the sole conduit through which an entire tribe's existence could be traced. The Maypure language would die out completely when the last parrot died. So Humboldt phonetically recorded the bird's vocabulary, though what he could discern from the birds constituted only traces of the language of the lost tribe.[1]

There are many other stories from around the world about unwritten languages lost when tribes died off, resulting in lost stories and entire histories and legacies of these groups.

There are six to seven thousand languages currently spoken in the world. It is estimated that 90 percent of these languages will become extinct in less than one hundred years from now.[2] With the loss of an average of one language every two weeks,[3] the world's language system has reached a crisis. In a little over thirty years from now, the majority of the languages spoken today around the globe will have been diluted or will have disappeared altogether.

## EXAMINATION OF THE ATMOSPHERE

It was my friend Jentezen Franklin who called my attention to this amazing text while we ministered in Israel. In Nehemiah 13:23–24, we read about how Nehemiah has returned to Jerusalem after the exile. As he is walking through the villages, undertaking an examination of the city around Jerusalem to which the exiled people of God are returning, he notices two unsettling things. First, the people of God have intermarried with pagans from the surrounding cultures—Ashdod, Ammon, and Moab. And second, he hears a strange language interspersed with Hebrew.

Every now and then, Nehemiah hears a Hebrew or Judean word mixed in with words of other languages. In other words, if a hearer speaks one of the languages but not the other, they can still speak and understand some of the words in a sentence. Much like with Spanish and Italian, or Portuguese and Spanish, some phrases are similar enough for Nehemiah to string together a basic meaning of a few sentences, but the Hebrew language is no longer the same.

Nehemiah realizes that the people can no longer speak the language of Judah. The very language in which God gave them the Law and with which He communicated and established relationship with them is disappearing, being diluted and mingled with foreign languages and cultures. For Nehemiah, this revelation was a dire warning.

The problem had nothing to do with ethnicity. The problem was about *language*. From Genesis to Revelation, there is no prohibition or warning against interracial marriage. In Scripture, the issue is never about color, race, or creed; it's always about spiritual diminishing. It's about intermarrying in the sense that when we come to other cultures and peoples who do not know Yahweh God, we run the risk of them influencing us away from Him more than we influence them toward Him.

Nehemiah is saying that the people can no longer speak or understand the language of Judah. He is concerned about the devaluation of the language of God and the resulting decline in talking God's language in the homes of the Israelites. This is important because it was the language of Judah with which God deposited His Law into His people. This means that if they can't talk the Law, then they can't walk the Law, behave the Law, speak the Law, and will no longer live by the Law of God. And the best way to scatter a nation, disperse her people, destroy their heritage, dilute their legacy, and water down their spiritual and religious values is to eliminate their unique communicational cohesion—their ability to *talk God talk*—both with Him and with one another.

It isn't necessarily about the way people talk in church, either, because blessings aren't just passed on Sunday morning from the pulpit and through the pews. It's about establishing an atmosphere of communication in terms of the presence of God no matter where we are, because He establishes relationships and affirms and communicates to us (whether verbalized or internal) through language.

Nehemiah knew that the establishment of an atmosphere of communication was crucial in the lives of God's followers. Because without a concise language, without a specific way of communicating with, interacting with, and developing relationship with one another and with God, any attempt to exchange thoughts, feelings, observations, cries of the heart, or shouts of joy would be nothing but noise.

## ESTABLISHMENT OF ATMOSPHERE

"These commandments that I give you today are to be on your hearts. Impress them on your children. Talk about them when you sit at home and when you walk along the road, when you lie down and when you get up" (Deuteronomy 6:6–7 NIV).

As the verses above tell us, the relationship between us and God is established in our hearts. Your relationship with God and the things He has planted and engraved on your heart are to be passed and transferred in the context of your home, your family, and your relationships.

God tells us to talk about these things when we walk along the road and anywhere else, to impress them on our children when we talk to them (and to anyone else), to talk about them when we lie down and when we get up. We are to pass on these commandments, these words of God. And that is done through speaking, through *language*.

In the book of Judges, we find that the generation that had received the Deuteronomy 6 instruction from God had failed. They had dropped the baton. The result was that the next generation didn't know who God was or what He had done. They barely even knew what Nehemiah was talking about, much less whom he was talking about. That generation did not know God, because one generation had the truth but didn't pass it on. No one had told them the story. The exiles' degraded ability to communicate had affected the most important things of their culture: their belief and their understanding of their heritage—who they were and who had birthed them.

Imagine all that had been lost due to their neglect and failure to pass a blessing forward. For example, God had once told the Israelites that wherever they went, they were to take with them the Ark of the Covenant of God. The Ark of the Covenant represented the presence of God. It was a symbol of their public worship when they gathered around the Ark. Who would explain that to the people now? Another important symbol given to the people had been that of circumcision, which was a mark on their bodies that symbolized the circumcision of their hearts. That information, too, was now gone. The Ark represented public worship, and the circumcision mark represented private witness, because there can't just be public worship alone, there must also be a personal witness and a change of heart. But the people had stopped the ritual of circumcision of their bodies, which in turn stopped their understanding of the importance of the circumcision of their hearts because nobody was there to communicate the importance of the two—the togetherness symbolism of being in the presence of God around the Ark and the personal witness symbolism of circumcision.

Many believers today have the worship part down, but they struggle in the witness area. They worship in the church, but when they go home they change their minds or forget what they've been taught or refuse to put what they've learned into play in their lives.

Paul commended Timothy on his faith, which had been passed on to him by his mother. And the faith of his mother had come from her mother, Timothy's grandmother. This is the generational blessing in the passing of faith. His grandmother taught and talked faith to his mother, and she taught and talked faith to Timothy. But if the people don't hear it, they can't talk it. And if they can't talk it, then the knowledge, the legacy, the stories—*everything*—is in danger of dying out like the language of the Maypure tribe on the Orinoco River in Venezuela.

What kind of talk are you talking in your family? What kind of talk are you allowing in your home? What kind of atmosphere of communication do you allow in your house? If you don't talk it, chances are pretty good they won't talk it. If you don't walk it, more than likely, they won't walk it. And the baton will be dropped and the race could be lost. All because of your neglect.

There are several dropped-baton communication dangers for us to be aware of. One of these dangers is "text talk," or sending text messages via a cell phone. According to one article, texting is a frequent disorder:

> Compulsive texting is a very frequent disorder. In fact, 23% of teens say they send and receive over 100 messages each day. 9% say they text compulsively. That's a lot of people. That's a total of 23 out of every 100 teens saying they send and/or receive *over* 100 messages *every day*. That's a lot of messages.[4]

Have you ever texted somebody whom you could just have easily talked to? For example, my wife and I were sitting together somewhere one afternoon and I texted her, and she texted me back. We were emulating the tendency of the new generation, which prefers substituting text talk in place of real talk.

Today's high-tech generation is developing an aversion to personal interaction. Previous generations didn't have that problem, but this generation is in danger of losing the dynamic of personal, face-to-face intimacy. My momma used to tell me, "Come here, so we can talk." She wanted to be close enough where she could look me in the eyes, where she could see my body language, where she could assess my reactions and weigh my words. She wanted to look at me so she could look *into* my heart.

We bless a generation through talk, through speaking with them. We need to beware of not allowing text talk to short-circuit the power of our personal interaction with others.

Another thing to be aware of is "unequal yoking." I could write a book on this topic, it's so foundationally important. We normally think of being unequally yoked as being between a believer and an unbeliever, and rightfully so. However, it's deeper than that. We think that as long as both people in a relationship are saved, everything will be fine. But we must also be aware of unequal *spiritual* yoking. Sometimes problems can arise when two Christians are on significantly different spiritual levels. A seasoned believer might have a challenge being "yoked" to a newly saved spiritual babe. When one person tries to create a home with someone who hasn't grown past the being baptized stage of walking with God, the issue is not just about position in Him; it's about a person's practices in life. And those *will* affect one or both people in the union at some point and might cause damage that is not easily disentangled.

An atmosphere is created in your home by what you allow into it. If you're a single person, it's perfectly fine if you live by yourself. But you'd better be real careful about who you allow into your home. You don't know what they're bringing into that environment. If you are trying to establish a holy ethos, a holy environment in your house, just as that holiness is created primarily by speaking blessings, it can all be undone by the introduction of an unholy element.

The challenge for us as believers is that when we are establishing a holy home and the person we are bringing into it doesn't understand the language of the holy, they are introducing the language of the unholy into that union. It's like the old demonstration of the two glasses: fill one glass with sparkling, clean water, and fill the other with muddied water. When you pour a bit of the clean water into the muddy water, you will notice that the muddiness remains without being noticeably cleaned up at all. But pour just a tiny amount of muddy water into the clean water and you will see that it instantly becomes visibly dirty and cloudy. The muddy affects the clean far more than the clean affects the dirty. It would take a lot of pouring clean into dirty before the clean takes over.

Unequally yoked is not just about being saved; it's about the values by which each person lives and speaks. This is because you are establishing an atmosphere not based on where you go to church, but based on the way you live and talk and walk. You create the climate of the house by your actions and your words. If you are talking holy talk and someone else is talking unholy talk, the climate of that house, the mixing of the holy with the unholy, will become muddied, dirtied, impure.

Nehemiah discovered that there was an entire generation that did not know the language of Judah. They did not know what God had done. And they did not know because no one had told them. The previous generation had dropped the ball, failed to pass the baton, didn't allow for the setting of an atmosphere of ongoing communication of the language, the values, the history, and the legacy of Judah.

## SET AN EXAMPLE OF ATMOSPHERE

I have a friend who is an Orthodox rabbi in a Jewish congregation. On Friday evenings, each member of the family invites someone else to come to Shabbat dinner at his house and they all gather around the meal. One Friday evening, I was an invited guest at their Shabbat meal in their home. The gathering was made all the more meaningful because they were joining together for the reading of a message that Jews around the world would read at Shabbat.

As I gazed about at the pictures of the children and grandchildren all around my friend's house, I realized that they didn't just learn the Law in their synagogue; they also learned in their home, around their table, at meals. The reading for that evening was from the book of Numbers, about Joshua and Caleb. The message was titled "Our Table Is Our Altar."

Do you have a table in your house, a place that is consecrated to God, where you also eat? Whom do you bring to that table? If you have a place where you go, and if you bring someone with you, are you all talking the same language while you are gathered together? Are you sharing the things of God with each other? These questions aren't just rhetorical.

There may be people in your life, perhaps from the next generation, who need the deposit of a word into their lives, their hearts, their spirits. It could be a son, a daughter, a nephew, a niece, a friend's child, or anyone who represents the next generation. Jesus said, "I only say the things I hear the Father say" (see John 12:49). Are your children speaking your language? What are your children hearing you say? What are they hearing you speak into their lives? What kind of kingdom values are you speaking that they might hear and learn? What kind of kingdom priorities do you talk about?

We have been sent out into the world to represent the kingdom. You might be a schoolteacher or a student, a businessperson or an assembly line worker, a pilot or an airline attendant. But are you a *kingdom* schoolteacher or student? A *kingdom* businessperson or assembly line worker? A *kingdom* pilot or airline attendant? As a Christian, you represent the kingdom of God to *everyone* you talk to. And you are called to share and communicate His kingdom with them no matter how strongly or obliquely, thereby passing the blessing to the next generation.

When Jesus was on His way to the cross, people kept insisting that Peter was one of those who had been with Jesus. Peter kept denying it, with increasing firmness. One of the times Peter denied it, he even did it with a curse at the woman.

But the Bible says Peter's speech betrayed him. I pray that my children's speech would betray them every time if they try to deny Jesus. I pray that their speech would reveal that they know Him. That little hesitation in their reply, that catch in their throat if they're asked about Him.

What you pour into your children and grandchildren will come out of them. I pray that you speak so much truth into them that they can't help but speak the truth. I pray that you call your children's names and their children's in prayer and bless them out loud. Speak blessings over them so all can hear.

Talk God talk to the generations coming up. And watch it spread.

## CHAPTER 4

# TOSS YOUR MANTLE

*"See, I will send the prophet Elijah to you before that great*
*and dreadful day of the LORD comes.*
*He will turn the hearts of the parents to their children,*
*and the hearts of the children to their parents."*

MALACHI 4:5–6 NIV

*And he will go on before the Lord, in the spirit and power*
*of Elijah, to turn the hearts of the parents to their children*
*and the disobedient to the wisdom of the righteous—*
*to make ready a people prepared for the Lord.*

LUKE 1:17 NIV

So many stories and stats we read reveal that fathers seem to be vanishing figures in American families. According to the National Fatherhood Initiative, 24 million children in America will go to bed tonight in a fatherless home. That's almost 25 percent of all children! According to this organization, compared to children raised in a home with both parents, kids raised in a home without a father are:

- more likely to have behavioral problems
- two times more likely to drop out of high school
- more likely to go to prison
- seven times more likely to become pregnant as a teen
- more likely to face abuse and neglect
- four times more likely to live in poverty
- more likely to abuse drugs and alcohol
- two times more likely to suffer obesity[1]

There are other studies as well. According to an article in the *Washington Times*, 11 percent of American children lived in homes without fathers in 1960. By 2012, in every state in the nation, the number of two-parent families had dropped significantly. Yet, even as the country added 160,000 families with children in the first decade of the new millennium, the number of two-parent households *decreased* by 1.2 million.[2] By 2012, the *Washington Times* story indicated, nearly one-third of US children were living without a father in their home. What a difference forty-two years had made—a staggering *tripling* of fatherless homes across the nation. The devil has been busy.

Vincent DiCaro, vice president of the National Fatherhood Initiative, stated in the *Washington Times* article, "America is awash in poverty, crime, drugs and other problems, but more than perhaps anything else, it all comes down to this: deal with absent fathers, and the rest follows." The *Washington Times* story also pointed out that "the spiral continues each year" because "married couples with children have an average income of $80,000, compared with $24,000 for single mothers." Mr. DiCaro added, "We have one class that thinks marriage and fatherhood is important, and another which doesn't, and it's causing that gap, income inequality, to get wider."

A Pew Research Center paper published a few years later backed up the premise of the *Washington Times* article, stating that "more and more children are growing up without a father in the home."[3] Clearly, fatherless homes with children in the family is a significant problem. Here are a few highlights from the Pew study:

- Just 57 percent of fathers say "parenting is extremely important" to their identity.
- Only 54 percent of dads report that "parenting is rewarding all of the time."
- Yet if you tweak the poll question a little bit, only 46 percent of fathers say that parenting is "*enjoyable* all of the time."
- Fathers reported spending, on average, only 8 hours out of every 112 waking hours each week caring for their

children, which means that a stunning 93 percent of their waking hours were spent *away* from childcare activities.

- Only 39 percent of fathers said they believe they are doing a "very good job" raising their children.

Although the Pew Research study pointed out that fathers today spend more time with their children than they did fifty years ago, it also indicated that the time spent isn't sufficient to provide these fathers' next generation of kids with what they will need to be emotionally nourished, secure, and prepared to pass their own baton of lessons, experience, and gained wisdom on to their own children someday—which means *that* generation will be left unprepared as well.

Another problem the Pew study revealed was that it has "become less common for dads to be their family's sole bread-winner." In 1970, 47 percent of couples with children were in families where only the dad worked. Yet, by halfway into the second decade of the new millennium, 73 percent of families with children had *both* parents working. And here's another not-so-surprising revelation from this study: about three-quarters of the public said having more women in the workplace "has made it harder for parents to raise children."[4]

So, what do the stats have to say about these challenging times for fathers who have children in their homes? Here are a few answers from the Pew study:[5]

- 52 percent of working dads say it is "very or somewhat difficult" to find a good balance of work and family life.
- 29 percent of working dads say they "always feel rushed."

- 48 percent of working fathers say they "would prefer to be home with their children, but that they need to work because they need the income."
- 49 percent of working dads say that "even though it takes them away from their families, they want to keep working."
- 53 percent of Americans say "mothers do a better job than fathers," yet (and brace yourself) only 1 percent of Americans say fathers "do a better job than mothers."
- 70 percent of adults say "it's equally important for new babies to bond with their mother and their father," yet only 2 percent say "it's more important for new babies to bond with their fathers."
- From 2016 to 2018, "among those who took time off to care for a new baby . . . fathers took a median of one week off from work." (To be fair to the fathers, the study also added that 49 percent of adults say "employers put more pressure on fathers to return to work quickly after the birth or adoption of a new child.")

I don't quote these statistics and studies to discourage the fathers among us—not at all. The vast majority of the fathers I've met who are unable to be with their children often enough, for whatever reason, dearly love their kids. But these statistics quoted above are shocking red flags, canaries in the often-difficult and always challenging "coal mines" of fatherhood and family responsibility. Still, these numbers bear out the extreme value of fathers in the home—good, solid, wise, committed, engaged fathers.

Let me encourage you working fathers reading this book to be aware of your position in the lives of your children: in your kids, you are creating *the future*, the next generation of people who will be running businesses and governments, taking care of the sick, employing people, setting government policy and public examples, and raising your grandchildren. Fatherhood is so vastly crucial in God's plan for family and passing the baton on to the next generation that to neglect your duties in this arena—no matter the reason—is not just to abandon your own children but your legacy and their future.

So, in seasons that sometimes seem to minimize the value of fathers, let me encourage you dads: hang in there! Stay with it! You are in the divine design in the mind of God. Steady the course. Be encouraged. The next generation needs you. You are the priest of your family. Don't go silent on them; be there for them; lead them well.

The last chapter in Malachi marks the beginning of four hundred years of silence from God's prophets, between the Old Testament and the New Testament. And then, after that break of four centuries, "reappearing" in the spirit and power of John the Baptist comes the mighty spirit of Elijah, the Old Testament prophet who marched through 1 Kings, took on vile leaders, performed miracles, displayed supernatural strength, and finally, as 2 Kings opens, was taken up to heaven in a chariot and whirlwind of fire—only to reappear more than six hundred years later in Matthew 17 with Christ at the transfiguration. Quite a résumé!

So the spirit of Elijah transcends that gap of four hundred years as God speaks in the Gospels of Matthew, Mark, Luke,

PASSING THE GENERATION BLESSING

and John. The prophetic word concerning John the Baptist was that when he comes, he will turn the hearts of the fathers to their children, and the hearts of the children to their fathers. The spirit of Elijah that was upon John the Baptist, the very Spirit of Jesus Christ Himself, would rebond fathers and children back with one another. That's good news (especially if its implementation isn't delayed too much longer!).

At the church where I am pastor, there's a young lady who never comes to services on Father's Day. She is a very active participant in ministry, but she can't bring herself to come to church on that particular day of the year because it dredges up such painful memories for her. It's one of those holidays that, for her, is a day that brings no celebration. Yet, in the Spirit, there is a move of God that has the power to turn the hearts of the children back to their fathers, and fathers to their kids. And that includes her. Because this spirit of Elijah, which rested on John the Baptist, is meant to bring *hearts* together. I don't know any dynamic of the personhood of God that manifests itself more than the truth that He can be a father to the fatherless, for if God is anything, He is first and foremost our Father.

The prophet Elijah is particularly known for passing the mantle. The highlight of his life, in fact, actually came at the end of his life. As a prophet, he wore a mantle, and as he was taken up in a whirlwind to heaven, he passed his mantle on to his spiritual son, Elisha. So, in this picture, Elisha is now seen as a father. The key of this passing of the mantle is the passing of blessing from one generation to the next. In passing the generational blessing, Elijah teaches us the principle of handing off the baton, of tossing our mantle, of passing all that we have gained spiritually into the next generation.

## YOU HAVE A MANTLE TOO

The Hebrew term for *mantle* refers to a wide, loose-fitting robe or outer garment. It has also been translated "cloak," "coat," and "garment." Thus, a mantle was basically a coat or cape, and the person wearing it was either a person of temporal authority, such as a royal personage, a military leader, or someone of religious importance such as a priest or prophet. In addition to being a coat, this outer cloak, this mantle, was a covering often worn functionally to keep the wearer warm and for protection from the elements. The mantle was essentially the only "blanket" the person had, so even when it was used as a pledge, the law required that the mantle be returned before bedtime.

When my son was a little boy, I use to wear a very well-worn, loose-fitting black leather jacket that was large enough to wrap him in it while I held him. On blustery days in Southern California, he would say, "Daddy, Daddy, the wind! Don't let the wind get me!" When the winds would blow, he felt safe, because he was in his daddy's mantle. He was covered and shielded from the elements.

From the idea of something that "covers" in the natural, a mantle represented a spiritual covering as well, and was usually referred to in terms of spiritual authority and anointing. Thus, Elijah's mantle was both a physical and spiritual covering. While it was represented by a physical garment, its spiritual covering came from God as a sort of "badge of authority" vested in Elijah so he could perform what God had called him to do. It was a "covering" that was transferable to Elisha and from him to John the Baptist. The mantle symbolizes the office of a prophet, as well as one's relationship with God—the *covering* of God. Think of it as a symbol of one's relationship being covered by, ordained by, and representative of God.

When Elijah ascended to the Father in a whirlwind, he tossed, threw, *cast* his mantle to his spiritual son, Elisha, who caught it. Just as in a relay race when you pass a baton, there is a split second when both people are holding the mantle. The difference is that the mantle is actually something you throw or toss to someone who will catch it. The dynamic of the spirit of Elijah was that he literally and intentionally tossed the mantle to Elisha (representing the next generation), who intentionally caught the garment, thereby figuratively deliberately cloaking him with the mantle of authority and responsibility to speak to his generation and into the next.

Two things have to happen in order to pass the mantle from one generation to the next: first, the present generation has to *release the mantle*; and second, the next generation has to *catch it*. This is very important. There must be an intentional release and an intentional receiving. The passing of the blessing is not just about the releasing from one generation; it is also about the *receiving* of the mantle by the next generation. There is continuity and a connection, where one generation releases and the next generation receives.

Likewise, when a father turns his heart to his children, it speaks of taking his position and accepting his role of spiritually covering his family.

## YOU HAVE A MANDATE

God is calling us fathers to be the spiritual covering over our families. Our family is to live under this covering, this mantle, which is first released by the turning of the hearts of fathers to their children, and the hearts of their children to their fathers. We, as fathers, must make a connection with our children—not a superficial connection but a heart connection. We are called in these last days to make a horizontal, personal connection within our homes so that our children will have a personal connection with us (their conduit with God) as well as a connection with the world. As fathers, we have a biblical mandate from God to be the heads, the leaders, the spiritual guides of our families.

Along with the honor that comes as head of the family, the father was expected to assume certain responsibilities. Those responsibilities were classified into three categories: social, economic, and spiritual. Let's look at them each.

- *Socially*, the father's responsibility was to ensure that no one took advantage of any member of his family. Additionally, the father was to provide his family with social relationships and connections.
- *Economically*, the father was to provide for the various needs of family members. Related to this were three specific duties: pass on an inheritance to the firstborn son, find his son a wife, and teach his son a trade.
- *Spiritually*, the father was responsible for the spiritual well-being of the family as a whole, as well as for the individual members of the family. In the earliest ages, the father functioned as the priest of his family, sacrificing on

their behalf. Later, when the priesthood was established in Israel, the father's spiritual role involved training his children in godliness.

The entire healing process begins with the work of the father in the household. First, God turns the hearts of fathers to their children. Then He turns the hearts of children to their fathers.

God's plan is to turn hearts and to revitalize homes through the spirit of Elijah. The spirit of Elijah can so affect the hearts of God's people that it can revolutionize the way they live in their homes. Reality, love, openness, and acceptance within the family are the proof of an authentic work of the Spirit. When fathers are awakened to their parental responsibilities, regenerated hearts will produce reprioritized lives, and reprioritized lives will produce redeemed families.

In Luke 1:17, the angel told Zechariah, the husband of Elizabeth (who was the cousin of Mary), that through the ministry of John the Baptist, there would be revival and renewal in the home:

> And he will go on before the Lord, in the spirit and power of Elijah, to turn the hearts of the parents to their children and the disobedient to the wisdom of the righteous— to make ready a people prepared for the Lord. (NIV)

John's reformed ministry was focused on our horizontal relationships with one another and on our vertical relationship with God. This means that John's ministry would bring families (horizontal relationships) together and would bring righteousness before God (our vertical relationship) back to the disobedient. The root of the solution, therefore, starts in the home. More than that, it starts with a relationship, with a covering, in the home, which gives us victory outside of the home in this messed-up culture today. It implies there has been a breach, a separation, and there is need for healing. It implies that respect is expected. It begins with hearts turning. The action of hearts turning toward one another implies reconciliation when that is needed. And it all begins with the father in the family.

As author M. Rutledge McCall stated it in his book *Slipping into Darkness*:

> It is from the top down that a family disintegrates. With each generation, fathers are more and more negligent in setting examples of the tenets of manhood to their boys. Honesty. Strength. Courage. Fairness. Faith. Love. Trustworthiness. Discipline. Sacrifice. Tenderness. Effort. Leadership. . . . Not a woman alive wouldn't happily and tirelessly follow a man possessing those qualities. But possessing and exercising those attributes consistently and with proper moderation isn't easy when we haven't been taught, when the foundation of example laid by our dads and grandfathers was weak or nonexistent. The blame may be theirs, but blame stops here and responsibility begins now. We need each other, us men, in order to care for our women and families properly, to teach, nourish, cherish, lead and love them.[6]

We as fathers must step up and take our rightful place. We are representatives of God the Father before our children and the world. God wants any distance between you and your father and between you and your children to be healed. For that, a spirit of Elijah must move in your heart, and a coming together must occur in the context of your vertical relationship with God.

The first scripture I learned was not "Jesus wept," the two-word verse most of my friends first learned. Rather, my parents taught us Exodus 20:12—"Honour thy father and thy mother: that thy days may be long upon the land which the LORD thy God giveth thee" (KJV). I never knew whether it was a promise or a threat! Note that it begins with honoring your parents ("honoring" speaks of an intentional connection). Even if your father has not been the best, this is not about him; it's about *honoring* him. God says honor your dad and it will add to your days, which means God will honor you as you honor your father. Sometimes in the realities of life, that can be a tough assignment.

I know a young lady whose mother and father were never married. In fact, her father married someone other than her mom. Her father never told his wife, his other kids, or any other family members about her. She is now in her thirties and is unknown to her father's side of her lineage. Although she has a quasi relationship with her father now in her adult years, she is also unknown by him beyond occasional brief meetings filled with superfluous chitchat. One of her greatest struggles has been to follow the mandate to honor her father. This verse is more than a nice little guideline; it can be a tremendous challenge when you put flesh on it and place it in the context of real-life situations that test our desire to honor God and His Word.

## YOU ARE THE MODEL

When Psalm 34:11 says, "Come, my children, listen to me; I will teach you the fear of the LORD" (NIV), the meaning of the word *teach* (same word we looked at in chapter 1 in Psalm 71) includes to "teach how to go to war," or "teach how to go into battle." The psalmist says, "I will teach you how to do battle in life," how to engage in warfare against the enemy, how to gain victory over him. This is because we physical beings here on earth are in spiritual warfare, yet we wrestle not against flesh and blood, which requires that we must use spiritual tactics to fight these spiritual battles. This means that when we fight against flesh and blood, we're fighting the wrong way, because the real fight is in the spirit realm. Thus, the psalm is actually saying, "Come and hear me, children, and I will teach you how to do warfare and the fear of the Lord."

"The fear of the Lord" is a two-sided coin. The word for *fear* means "respect" or "reverence"; to "be restrained." The psalm is saying, "I will teach you how to respect and revere God." This is interesting, because most of us, in many cases, learn more about God from mothers than we do from our fathers. Yet the pattern throughout Scripture is that dads are the ones responsible for spiritual education. There's something that children can learn about their relationship with God by observing their relationship with us fathers: how to have reverence for God, honor God, respect God.

I'm amazed at the way some children speak to their parents, and even more so at how some older kids talk to their parents. I've heard people—young and not so young—curse in the presence of their mother (something that some of us learned the hard way is a great way to get a taste of the bathroom bar of soap or, worse, a swat on the rear). Just as there are some things we allow and don't allow to be said or done in our houses, there's a standard of honor and respect we must display toward the Lord.

The word for *fear* doesn't speak only of reverence, but also of *restraint*. When we have a high regard for God, we restrain ourselves from living certain ways and from doing certain things, because of the respect and reverence we have for God. That reverence for our Lord restrains us; there are things we cannot and will not do. Out of our respect for Him we draw a line we never cross.

There are things you should never do. Not because they wouldn't feel good, but because you fear breaking God's heart. Ask yourself this: are there things you refuse to do because you honor God? Are there some places you don't dare go, simply because you don't want to dishonor God?

In the wilderness when the devil was tempting Jesus to worship him, he said, "All this I will give you . . . if you will bow down" (Matthew 4:9 NIV). The tense of the word *bow* in Greek is *aorist*, which speaks of an action at a point in time. So, use your sanctified imagination. The setting is in the wilderness. There is no one out there but Jesus and the devil. Eyeball to eyeball. Devil playing chicken with the Creator of the universe. Devil says, "Jesus, I'll give You all the kingdoms of the world . . . and all You gotta do is bow to me [in the aorist tense] just one time." He's saying, "Look around, Jesus: there's nobody here. It's just You 'n' me. If You don't tell, I won't tell. Just take a quick knee." But Jesus resists, for one reason only: because He knows *He* alone is the King of kings, to whom everybody will bow down one day.

Not the other way around. But most of all, such a thing would dishonor the Father.

There are some things I can't do because of reverence for God. There are other things I can't do because of restraint. These are the things we must teach our children as we toss the mantle to them. As we are assured in Proverbs 22:6, "Train up a child in the way he should go, and when he is old he will not depart from it" (NKJV).

We've learned that hearts are turned through teaching and through training. This means if you point your children in the right direction, they can only wander off so far. If you put them on the right road, they will *be* on the right road. I must admit that passages like this challenge me, and I end up taking them by faith. I acknowledge that it is a spiritual principle and not a formula with a guarantee. I really can't explain the seemingly contradictory examples of this passage. For instance, siblings raised in the same house, under the same rules, in the same godly atmosphere with righteous values and standards, sometimes go opposite ways. However, I am equally baffled and pleasantly surprised when I see multitudes of wayward prodigals make their way back to the house of the Father after having wasted years in the far country.

Some of us know what it's like to try to put our children on the right road while also acknowledging that they still have to make their own choice to follow that road. Let me pause here and admonish you: don't let the devil put you on a guilt trip because things didn't turn out the way you wanted concerning your children. It's not your job to do it for them. Your job is to show them how to do it, to direct them, to lead them to the right road so they may choose the right way. If you start them off in the right direction, on the right road, during their formative years, and don't deviate throughout their lives by giving them confusing or contradictory messages or examples, then they'll know the right way and will make their own decisions. And in the end, it will be their decisions that will impact their lives.

We train *with* our children, but we can't train *for* them.

We walk *with* them and we guide them, but we can't *do it* for them.

Your child is going to fall. Your child is going to make mistakes, but all they need to know is that you will be there when they fall. When they stumble, when they fall to their knees, just let them know you are there for them. Just as Jesus lets you know He is there for you when you falter, your kids need to know you will be there when they fall. Never forget: their generation is *your* legacy.

## CHAPTER 5

# LEARN
# TO LISTEN

*Elias was a man subject to like passions as we are,*
*and he prayed earnestly that it might not rain:*
*and it rained not on the earth by the space*
*of three years and six months. And he prayed again,*
*and the heaven gave rain, and the earth*
*brought forth her fruit.*

JAMES 5:17–18 KJV

My mother used to say to me, "Boy, you are gonna learn to listen to me." Sometimes she'd say it in warning, and other times in encouragement that I would one day learn to trust her about God. Sometimes it was when I was fearful, or during times when the Lord had told her something for me or about me.

As we have studied so far, the idea of passing blessings is highlighted in the life of Elijah. The mighty prophet is spoken of in the book of James as an example from whom James learned to listen to the voice of God, because of the power God gave to Elijah as he performed God's will. Elijah is lifted up as a model of passing blessings from one generation to the next because he not only listened to God but also heeded God's words. The lesson is that blessings, such as rainfall coming after a three-year drought, cannot be passed on until we learn to *listen* to God and respond to Him. Only then, when we hear and heed, can we participate in His blessings.

In Luke 1:17 (which makes reference to Malachi 4:5–6), Luke likens Elizabeth's son, John the Baptist, to the great prophet Elijah, in whose power and spirit Luke says John came "'to turn the hearts of the fathers to the children,' and the disobedient to the wisdom of the just, to make ready a people prepared for the Lord" (NKJV).

This passage speaks of both a generational connection (the generation of the times) and of a transgenerational connection (a future generation). Elijah is lifted up as one who has passed a blessing to John the Baptist. Yet, in fact, Elijah passed his anointing on to his spiritual son, Elisha (which is symbolic of passing the blessing from one generation to the next), and now Elisha stands as a model of passing a blessing from one generation to the next. So the blessing went from God to Elijah, from Elijah to Elisha, from Elisha to John . . . and eventually on to us today, and so forth into future generations, through the teachings and learning of Elijah.

## LISTENING:
## THE KEY TO THE BLESSING

The spirit of Elijah is a demonstration of the three dimensions of passing a blessing: God spoke *through* him, God spoke *to* him, and God spoke *with* him. Sometimes God will speak a blessing to you; sometimes you speak to the Lord, requesting blessing; and sometimes the Lord will speak a blessing through you. However, in order for it all to take place in accordance with God's plan and God's will, you must always be able to hear the blessing spoken, because one of the ways God passes a blessing to you is by pronouncing it through His Word.

We learn two truths and lessons from the revelation of the life of Elijah (and from the related revelation in the book of James) that pertain to generational blessings: the first is that God wants to use us; the second is that God wants to speak to us. In other words, God wants to bless you, but you will neither know He wants to bless you nor will you know what His blessings are until you acquire the spiritual disciplines of *learning to hear His voice* and *listening to Him*.

Blessings released by God in the form of His word must also be received. Thus, the blessing is made effective by recognizing, hearing, and responding to the word of blessing. Just as the key to *receiving* a blessing is listening and hearing the blessing, the spirit of passing a generational blessing is key in the *releasing* of a blessing into the life of another. In other words, there is a spirit connected with the recognition and acceptance of passing blessings forward. This spirit rested upon Elijah just as it rested on John the Baptist.

Have you ever been used by God to speak a word of blessing to a young person who heard you and believed you? If so, you passed on and released a blessing from your generation to another.

## GOD WANTS TO USE YOU

When we look at the life of Elijah in this topic of passing a generational blessing, the first truth you need to understand is that *God wants to use you.*

James 5:17 describes Elijah as "human just like us" (MSG). One version says he was "a human being" (NIV). Another version says he was "as human as we are" (NLT). The English Standard Version says he "was a man." This means that Elijah was a man—not an angel, not a seer or a clairvoyant, diviner, or mystic. Not a super saint. Not one of God's Green Berets. Just a man.

That sounds counterintuitive, because here's a man whom God used mightily. A man whose blessing, whose power, whose influence literally touched a nation and changed a generation. In the end, he never even died; he went bodily to heaven in a fiery chariot. God used him in mighty ways, yet James strives to make clear to us that this man whom God used mightily was just an ordinary person like you and me.

That is a significant and profound message for us today.

James is seeking to dispel a common Jewish belief at the time that prophets were in a different category. The thinking was that they were special, a breed apart, from a different realm. But James says, no, you've got it all wrong, people. Elijah was just a regular person, a human being just like us.

The phrase "just like us" is a compound word in the Greek language. The prefix is *homo*, which means "same"; and the root word is *pathe*, which means "emotion" or "passion." James is saying that this mighty prophet of God had passions and emotions just like us. He had feelings just like us. He had similar struggles and vicissitudes. He went through the same kind of stuff we experience. He was even a guy who sometimes became afraid, a man who was weak and insecure, just like us. At times he felt sorry for himself, just like us. Yet, God used him mightily. That should be a comforting and empowering message for us. We're no different than Elijah, for he, too, was "a man subject to like passions as we are" (James 5:17 KJV).

God often uses people just like you and me. He surrounds Himself with people who have rarely, if ever, been great. He looks for the misfits and the geeks, the inexperienced and the unskilled, the recently laid-off and the unemployed. He looks for the professionals and the executives, the PhDs and the MDs. God chooses whom He will. He's not looking for great people or fine people or perfect people or the smartest or strongest or most skillful people. He looks for regular, everyday Janes and Joes to do great things. The disciples learned this. Jesus told them to "go into all the world" (Mark 16:15 NIV). But knowing their tendency to sometimes break out like bulls in a china closet, He told them to wait. Hold up! Slow your roll! They were just ordinary people. They were regular guys.

Several years ago, the late Danniebelle Hall, a protégé of the late gospel singer/songwriter Andraé Crouch, declared in her song "Ordinary People" the truth of how God uses all kinds of people to accomplish His will: It makes no difference how insignificant we feel or how the best we can offer seems so small, "because little becomes much as you place it in the Master's hand."[1]

God uses people who are willing to take up the mantle, grab the baton, and do what He asks of them. You need to be on the lookout for opportunities God will give you to bless others. As Booker T. Washington stated, "Opportunity is like a bald-headed man with only a patch of hair right in front. You have to grab that hair, grasp the opportunity while it's confronting you, else you'll be grasping a slick bald head."[2]

In Ephesians 2:10, Paul talks about who we are—"his workmanship, created in Christ Jesus unto good works, which God hath before ordained that we should walk in them" (KJV). The New Living Translation says, "We are God's masterpiece." Yet, we are regular, ordinary people, God's handiwork, created in Christ Jesus to do good works that He has prepared in advance for us to do.

The word *created* means "carefully created or brought into being." In other words, there's no accident to your life. God says your life is a masterpiece. Once you get that in your head and don't buy in to the world's lie that you're something less than who God says you are, then you are on your way to doing and being what God has called you to do and to be. It's much like a parent with a child. We don't shape character in our children just by telling them what to be. We don't shape character by telling them what they can be, what they ought to be, or what they already are. We shape character in our children merely by telling them who created them. We tell them God loves them and that He has invested Himself in them. We give them truth, hope, reality. And we live out that model for them to see and to follow.

You are a masterpiece, I don't care what you've been through or where you come from. And it's not me telling you that; it's God saying it. So, if you're sitting anywhere near a mirror or a window as you read these words, look at your reflection and tell yourself: "The God who created me says I'm a masterpiece!" Might be a masterpiece in the making, but He carefully and lovingly created you because He has a plan for your life that will bring Him glory. And as long as you show up each day ready to do His will, He will bring His plan forth in your life.

I don't care what you are going through right now. I don't care how hard things seem. I don't care how dark it looks in your life. If you understand one thing in your life, understand this: *God still has His hand on you.* If you will yield to it, He can use you, because you are a God-blessed masterpiece. And once you get it in your mind and in your spirit that you are God's masterpiece, you won't let the world tell you anything different from that.

So tell yourself, "I am a masterpiece." Make sure you handle yourself like you are a masterpiece, too, and demand that other folks handle you like you are a masterpiece. Don't let them treat you like some piece of throwaway junk. God has put His hand on you. He put His glory and stamp on you, and you are His masterpiece. Not in arrogance, but in confidence, know this:

that He who began a good work in you shall be faithful to complete it.

Get it into your spirit that God wants to use you. If you're sitting next to somebody as you read these words, then surprise them: turn to them and say out loud, "You know, you're sitting next to a masterpiece; you are sitting next to a miracle." And after their initial surprise, tell them how God wants to create a masterpiece in them, too, if they're willing to yield their lives to His will.

I could spend the rest of this book telling you what God has brought me through. God surrounds Himself with inadequacy. He hangs out in the context of inability. He specializes in folks who think they can't. And, in fact, they actually *can't*—not until He puts His hand on them. You can do all things through Christ, who strengthens you, because God wants to use you. Let that simmer and cook into you for a moment. It matters not your situation, your age, or your category in life. God wants to use you.

## GOD CONVERSES

Here's the next thing God wants to do with you: He wants to speak to you. Now don't tune me out. I'm not talking about weird stuff. I'm not talking about hearing voices and talking to invisible, imaginary people. I want you to get this. We often make two mistakes in this area of God speaking: we categorize other Christians as those who hear God speak to them, and we disqualify ourselves as candidates for hearing God speak to us. Some people say, "Well, God speaks to him, and God speaks to her, and God uses him, and God uses her. But He wouldn't speak to me. He's never spoken to me. Matter of fact, let me text her to find out what He said to her to say to me, 'cause He surely wouldn't speak to me."

*Wrong!*

Our great, big God wants to speak to "li'l ol' you." And it's not just that God wants to speak to you; He wants to speak *with* you, converse with you. The key to Elijah's life, the man who passed on the generational blessings, is that he learned both sides of the dynamic of prayer: God spoke *to* him and *with* him. And through his two-way conversations with God, Elijah spoke to his generation (read the book of 1 Kings to see all of the powerful words this mighty prophet passed on to the generation), and he spoke into the next generation through Elisha, who spoke to his generation (read 2 Kings for Elisha's ministry of passing on generational blessings), and so on throughout future generations. Their conversations with God reverberated and revealed God's Word right up to today as you read the words and teachings of these great patriarchs of the faith.

Elijah teaches us both sides of prayer. First, the Bible says he prayed he spoke to God. The dynamics of prayer are multidimensional. It's God using you as a voice and a vessel for His Word, and it's you becoming a channel for the Word of God. It is more talking *with* God than talking *at* God. It's you talking to God, God talking to you, you and God talking with each other, and God talking through you to others.

Prayer is not a monologue. Prayer is not going to God with your laundry list. Prayer is not the nightly news report. You don't go to God and say, "Hey, guess what?" He already knows *what*, now He wants to talk with you about it. Prayer is not God talking to you, and prayer is not just you talking to God. Prayer is you talking *with* God. That is the example of Elijah.

## GOD ANSWERS

Elijah prayed a big prayer. We learn in James 5:17 that the prayer was that it would not rain. That is one king-sized ask. (If you're going to pray, why not go big?) And when Elijah prayed that it would not rain, it did not rain for forty-two months. Big prayer, big result.

Then, in the next verse, he prayed that it would rain—another big prayer, after such a long drought. And after he prayed that it would rain, it rained. Pray a big prayer, get a God-sized answer.

"Shut off the water, Lord!"

*BAM*—no rain, three and a half years.

"Okay, back on now, Father!"

*WHAM*—rain all over the place.

When the mighty in faith open their mouths to pray, buckle up, because miracles are about to pour forth.

When you pray, you need to remember to whom you are praying. If you ever realize how big the God is to whom you pray, you'll understand that it's inconsistent to pray little prayers to your great big God. If you have a little God, your little prayer will fit your little God. Elijah realized that he wasn't just praying to a little *might* god, he was praying to the *Almighty* God. When you realize how big your God is, when you understand the power of your big God, you will ask big things, because through

Him you will understand that you can do big things. Spending time in conversation with God is what teaches us to learn to trust our big God.

Have you ever tried to do something so big that you couldn't do it without God? If you can do what you're trying to do without God, it's probably not big enough. You need something that if God doesn't pull it through, it will never come through. You need something that if God doesn't do it, it will never get done. You need some goals that without the hand of God reaching in, you'll never reach them. It takes no more breath to say, "Lord, help me to do average," than it does to say, "Lord, help me to do something really big!" This is how I live my life: I would rather shoot and miss doing something big for God than succeed at doing little or, worse, experiencing nothing because I asked nothing of Him.

For example, if you believe you are a global leader, you must first realize you serve a God in a global context. If you can ever get a global mind-set, you will realize that what God has put in you is much greater than the context in which you find yourself. So He gives you a global vision to be a global leader in this global world.

I have a son in the ministry who pastors a church in Johannesburg, South Africa. Theo Muka's church is located in Hillbrow. Okay, let me help you understand Hillbrow. Think of the most dangerous, gang-infested, drug-filled, prostitute-roaming areas you can. Now wrap them all up and put them all together and you get an idea of the part of Johannesburg I'm talking about. Yet, in this part of town, drug addicts have been delivered. Prostitutes have been saved. Gang members have given their lives to the Lord. All through his ministry right smack-dab in the middle of all this stuff going on. However, on Sundays he sees maybe only two or three hundred people. But please, please don't gauge the effectiveness of his ministry by the size of his weekly audience. God has used him in the Congo, Great Britain, and Germany. Because his vision is far, far greater than what you might see on Sunday morning. It's far grander than where he stands every week. He recognizes the greatness of his great God. He prays big prayers, and God uses him in magnificent, miraculous, magnanimous ways. He has big faith in an even bigger God. And he's just a little guy too! Maybe five foot four or five five. But he learned something about God and about prayer: if you ever realize how big your God is, it will impact how big your prayers are.

Have you ever wanted God to use you someplace you've never even seen? Maybe you have a passion to go into the mission field in a place you've only read about. God has planted in your spirit that He wants to use you over there. He's going to take you there, because He would not show it to you if He didn't plan to use you there. You've got to speak it. Prepare yourself. Study. Learn the skills you need. Trust God to give you favor with the right people. Be on the lookout for the open door. Then go pack your bags.

When God speaks to you, it is in the greatness of His majesty. God's word to us today is that we can't even begin to imagine the things He wants to do in us and through us. *If you let Me speak to you*, He says, *I'll show you how to go where you've never been*. If God has placed a dream in you, what He has placed in you He is going to bring out of you. And He's going to take all of the glory for Himself. God can take you higher than you have ever been before to do things you never imagined before.

When I was a little boy, my daddy told me something I didn't fully grasp until I was grown. He said, "Son, aim for the stars. And if you miss the star, at least you'll land somewhere in the atmosphere of a star." And that's a whole lot higher than where you started.

God is a great God. So why not pray great prayers?

## GOD WHISPERS

The other side of prayer is learning to hear God's voice. In 1 Kings 19:11, what gets Elijah's attention is not when "a great and powerful wind tore the mountains apart and shattered the rocks before the LORD" (NIV). Nor is Elijah overly excited when "after the wind there was an earthquake" (NIV). And it didn't impress him much when, in 1 Kings 19:12, "after the earthquake came a fire" (NIV). Elijah had seen God do a lot of things in his days as a prophet of God. These displays were not really a big deal for the Creator of the universe, and Elijah knew that. No, what really got the mighty prophet's attention came in 1 Kings 19:12: "And after the fire came a *gentle whisper*" (NIV, emphasis mine).

There was a ferocious wind. But God was not in the wind. There was a massive earthquake. But God wasn't in the earthquake. There was a raging fire. God wasn't there either. Instead, what really got Elijah's attention was when he heard the Almighty's gentle whisper. Astounding.

Here's the message: our God, who does big and mighty things, often whispers. It's as though He refuses to compete with the cacophony of sounds that bombard our senses. And in the midst of the raging storms and earthquakes, fires, and dangers that swirl around us, God waits for things to calm down. Then He speaks in a still, small whisper.

God is whispering; He's not shouting. And His whisper is always profound.

Elijah had gone to the brook in the Kerith Ravine because the evil King Ahab and his wicked wife, Jezebel, had come to power and were wreaking havoc throughout Israel. So Elijah pronounced three years of drought throughout the land, and God instructed him to hide out in the Kerith Ravine, east of the Jordan. And it was there at that brook where Elijah learned to really trust God, because it was through that brook that God fed him and provided for him.

Elijah had gone to the brook in obedience, and there he had water. But after the rains stopped, so did the brook. The place he had gone for blessing was no longer a blessing. It had only been a blessing for a season. Now it was time to move on. So, in 1 Kings 17:9, God told Elijah, "Go"! (NIV). *Don't stay here any longer.* This place is shriveling up!

What you want from the brook is not coming. What you need is no longer coming from the brook that gave you what you needed for a season. If the season you've been in is over, without the provision God is going to give you next, you will wither where you are now. So, it's time to get on up out of there. Maybe that's the word of the Lord to you. That job is a dead-end street. Where you want to go, that position will not take you. The life in that relationship you're in will not produce the life you need, because that brook has gone bone-dry. It's time to leave. The season for that stopover is over. What you need, this thing can no longer supply. The longer you stay at this stop, the more time you're wasting, because if you don't leave this place, you'll never get what God is trying to pour into your life.

When God says leave, what do you do? Simple: *you leave!*

So, Elijah leaves. He goes to the top of Mount Carmel, where he takes on 450 prophets of an idol god. And he wins. After that, a vicious woman by the name of Jezebel, wife of evil King Ahab, vows to kill Elijah. So how does Elijah, this regular guy, human just like you and me, with normal emotions just like us, react when he's threatened by a psychotic killer queen? He gets scared! He hightails it out of there, scampers like a rabbit from a bobcat. He runs from one woman. Mighty prophet Elijah hits the road as if a college debt collector is after him with a pistol.

Elijah goes and hides in a cave. And there, in 1 Kings 19:9, the mighty Elijah the Tishbite is hunkered down, shivering from fright, scared witless of this woman, when God suddenly speaks to him.

"'Lijah? What in the world are you doing here, man, hiding in fear like this?"

Consumed by insecurities and doubt, Elijah is having his own little pity party of one. He says, "I'm the only one left, Lord! I'm out here all by myself—and she's one dangerous, mean ol' gal, God!"

"Go back your way," God tells him.

This doesn't mean to go back the way he came. It means *go back to who you are.* God is telling Elijah, "You're better than this! You're more than this. Why are you hiding in this cave in fear and trepidation? Why do you think I have abandoned you? Why do you think I've turned my back on you when I just brought you through 450 prophets of Baal? Don't you think I can handle this one woman? I'm waiting on you to man up and come out of that cave, 'Lij!"

*What are you doing cowering here? This is not who you are!*

Has God ever asked you why you are settling into your own private little cave? What are you doing here? You're better than that. God has bigger plans for your life than that little hole. The anointing that is on you is too big for that dinky cave. The power and destiny He has for you is too big to be holed up in that hovel. Step out of the shack and step up on His Word. And watch God use you. Go back to being who He designed you to be. He still wants to use you.

The word of the Lord came to Elijah, *If you stay where you are, judgment is coming.* The word of God said, *That brook is dry, so move on.* What you need will never come from where you are. The brook was bone-dry and this cave is too small! I have bigger plans for you!

Maybe as you're reading these words, you're recalling how God has gotten in your ear, into your spirit, like never before. "For what I want to do in your life," God is telling you, "that cave you're in is too small."

He's whispering to you, "Come. Your fear and self-pity are too tiny."

He's whispering, "What are you doing here? Leave!" What you need is not coming from that brook! That brook is dry! Move on! You have mighty things to do! You've got bigger things to pass on to the next generation than whatever you think you have in your little cave.

So, *go!*

## CHAPTER 6

# PRAY
# FOR THEM

*The hearts of the people cry out to the Lord.*
*You walls of Daughter Zion, let your tears flow*
*like a river day and night; give yourself no relief,*
*your eyes no rest. Arise, cry out in the night,*
*as the watches of the night begin; pour out your heart*
*like water in the presence of the Lord.*
*Lift up your hands to him for the lives of your children,*
*who faint from hunger at every street corner.*

LAMENTATIONS 2:18–19 NIV

God has a two-prong strategy for blessing the next generation. It involves prayer and penetration. How do we get into and impact the next generation? We pray for the children, and we penetrate the culture.

As we seek to learn how to pass along a generational blessing, we need the input and help of two more prophetic voices. We have examined the life of the prophet Elijah. Now let's move on to Jeremiah, the prophet from the house of Hilkiah, his father. As a little boy, Jeremiah saw the hand of God reaching out and touching his mouth (Jeremiah 1:9). Jeremiah speaks around about 586 BC during a time when Israel was nearing the end of Babylonian captivity after the army had desolated and burned Jerusalem.

Jeremiah speaks of the time of the exile, when despair, famine, and destitution filled God's land and His people. Jerusalem is but a ravaged memory of dust and rubble. Jeremiah writes of his painful concern for the next generation, and calls the people of God to pass blessings on to them. He speaks of the responsibility one generation has to the next to tell them about the goodness, the judgment, and the faithfulness of God.

Jeremiah wrote at least two books of the Bible, including the one that bears his name. The other book, Lamentations (the book of weeping or the book of lament), is traditionally accepted as having been written by him as well. The book of Lamentations contains five funeral songs that express the people's grief over the fall of Judah and the destruction of the dearly loved city of

Jerusalem. The songs describe the horrible devastation and cruelty Jeremiah saw. The songs acknowledge that sin brought God's judgment, and they look beyond the present agony to see a God of faithfulness and mercy who is able to restore the nation.

Lamentations is a book of pain. Jeremiah is often referred to as the "weeping prophet" because he openly wept over the sins of the nation. He cried as he bore the painful burden of the godless behavior of the people of his time. Yet Jeremiah also wrote words of comfort and encouragement. For example, in Jeremiah 29:11 he recorded, "'For I know the plans I have for you,' declares the LORD, 'plans to prosper you and not to harm you, plans to give you hope and a future'" (NIV). He also wrote in Lamentations 3:22–23, "Because of the LORD's great love we are not consumed, for his compassions never fail. They are new every morning; great is your faithfulness" (NIV).

There's also another man, a modern-day "prophet" of sorts, who comes along in 1971. He's from the house of Gaye, and his name is Marvin. No less a spokesman of his time, with discernment and observational skills as he commented on the generation of his day, Marvin Gaye looked out upon the cataclysmic catastrophes of the culture more than four decades ago. Jeremiah the prophet may have wept, and Elijah may have fought, but this modern-day prophet, Marvin Gaye, simply raised a question as he looked with similar generational discernment as Jeremiah did in many ways. I suggest there is a connection between these two cultural giants from different eras.

Marvin Gaye asked a musical paraphrase of the plight of Jeremiah when he posed the profound prophetic question as a song lyric: "What's going on?" Marvin wanted to save the children. He heard the divine call to take dominion over creation and manage it. He recognized that God gave a divine command to humanity to manage and govern itself. And he wondered, "Mercy, mercy me, what's happening to the ecology?" He was saying, "What has happened to God's creation?" What's going on?

Don't miss that insightful question while you're jamming and partying to the melodic musical styling of this modern-day prophet. There is significant substance to the revelation of a contemporary prophet. Marvin peered into the cataclysmic condition of the collective inner-city communities of society and prophetically saw the crumbling state of humanity.

Marvin was not a perfect man by any means. He needed healing, like many of us do. He just didn't always know where it came from. Still, the substance of his 1971 song "Inner City Blues (Make Me Wanna Holler)" reflects our present-day culture as he sings about increasing crime rates, police shootings, setbacks, high taxes: "God knows where we're heading / Oh, make me wanna holler."[1]

These words were sung going on nearly half a century ago by Marvin Gaye, who looked at the culture and society much like Jeremiah did in his time. Likewise, Jeremiah had looked at the plight of the culture and he, too, had become frustrated, because no one listened to his words. Jeremiah had a "church" where no one was saved, and he cried out to God, "No one listens to me," much like the sentiment Marvin expressed.

Jeremiah suffered from a spiritual depression, because he saw no fruit in the seeds he was sowing. People mocked him when he talked about sin. He examined the things that were happening in his time and was so frustrated that over and over again he wanted to give up. Just throw up his hands and call it a day. *Make me wanna holler.*

When you look around and observe the plight and predicament in our shifting society, do you ever want to just give up on it all? Look at the present generation, look at the culture, at the schools, at the financial system, the government, the elected politicians, the bureaucracy, the so-called leaders. If you look close enough, it will make you want to holler.

Jeremiah and Marvin meet on the common ground of concern for the children. These two prophets, separated by millennia, come together on the topic of anxiety about kids. Jeremiah writes Lamentations as he sees what lies ahead for the children. He sees the potential destruction of a whole generation and calls the people of God to respond. He not only looks at the present generation, he also sees the next generation and realizes the danger of what's being inherited and passed down to them. He recognizes that the nation is just one generation away from extinction. So he speaks about the priority of the children, the next generation.

Marvin, on the other hand, sang of an intimate personal healing. He didn't know that only God could heal him. He took to the dance floor saying, "Got to Give It Up." Yet, he also said, "Don't go and talk about my Father . . . Jesus is my friend."

Neither Jeremiah nor Marvin was a perfect man. Both had flaws of frailty. Both could be classified as spiritual schizophrenics. Jeremiah wanted to die. He suffered from depression. During his ministry, there were no spiritual converts. Yet, they met at the crossroads of the destiny between their generation and the next. And in their humanity, they had urgent concerns to impart to the people of God.

## CONCERN FOR THE CHILDREN

The last part of the final sentence in Lamentations 2:22 says, "those I cared for and reared my enemy has destroyed" (NIV). In this verse, the prophet is saying that these are the ones he raised and cared for. This conjures the idea of a parent raising up a child. He is saying, "My children that I cared for have been destroyed by my enemy!"

As we are called and challenged with a responsibility to the next generation, the prophet tells us to consider the condition of the children.

The world is moving so fast now. For instance, one of the fastest-declining arts is the art of writing. Some people are trying to reverse this trend. When kids go to summer camps, they aren't allowed to take any devices with them; they have to write to their parents every week by hand. But the counselors are discovering that many kids don't even know how to write. An article in the *Guardian* titled "The Lost Art of Handwriting" states, "Technology seems to have ruined our collective handwriting ability. The digital age, with its typing and its texting, has left us unable to jot down the simplest of notes with anything like penmanship. A third of us can't even read our own writing, let alone anyone else's, according to a survey by the not-entirely-unbiased print and post specialists Docmail."[2]

Another example of this fast-moving world in rapid decline is one of propriety and modesty. Last time I went out dancing, we were doing the Bump, then came the Mashed Potato, followed by the Jerk and the James Brown! (I'm smiling as I'm writing—LOL! Most of you have *no* idea what those dances were!) A few years later, people started doing the Running Man. Nowadays they're twerking—an overtly sexual imitation done openly, in public, and without shame. I fear the sins of the previous generations' parents are being manifested as consequences against the children. Parents are reaping a whirlwind from neglecting the lives of their children, the greatest resource of humanity.

All of this is affecting how religion is viewed by this generation and the next. A 2014 Pew Research Center report says the fastest-growing "religious" groups are the agnostic, the atheist, and the nonaffiliated. In this poll, religious "nones" is shorthand used to refer to people who self-identify as atheists or agnostics, as well as those who say their religion is "none in particular." These "nones" now make up roughly 23 percent of the US adult population—a stark increase from 2007, when 16 percent of Americans claimed to be nones. During that same period, when the nones increased from 16 to 23 percent (nearly a 50 percent increase), the Christians and church-affiliated group fell from 78 to 71 percent (almost a 10 percent decrease). Of the millennials (people born between 1981 and 1996), 35 percent are nones. In addition, the nonaffiliated as a whole are getting even younger: the median age of nonaffiliated adults is now thirty-six, down from thirty-eight years old in 2007, and significantly younger than forty-six, the overall median age of US adults in 2014.[3]

These shocking statistics point to the spiritual destruction of a generation. When the fastest-growing religious group in the country are the nones, and when Christians and church-affiliated groups are in steady decline, we are in danger of losing a generation.

Nones have also made more gains through religious switching than any other group analyzed in the study. Only about 9 percent of US adults say they were raised without a religious affiliation; among this group, roughly half say they now identify with a religion (most often Christianity). Yet, nearly one in five Americans (18 percent) have moved in the other direction, saying that they were raised as Christians or members of another faith, but now have no religious affiliation (the groups in relative decline are Christianity, Islam, and Scientology—which doesn't qualify as a religion, but more of a "personal process").[4] This means that for every person who left the ranks of the nonaffiliated and became a Christian, more than four people became nones. Let that sink in for a moment. It means that an entire generation of Christians are actively abandoning their faith in comparative droves.

In his day, Jeremiah said in Lamentations 2:20 (NIV), "Look!" This is an urgent call for justice, a call for mercy. Jeremiah is asking God to have mercy on this people, who are living in an unrighteous culture. He's saying *the children are in trouble!*

In these last days, we must consider the condition of the children. Because if Jeremiah was right about the enemy destroying the children's generation way back then, I've got a news flash for you: it's even worse now, folks.

## CRY OUT!

Children are the future generation. This is why the prophet Jeremiah speaks of the priority of the children. He says the children have been duped by false prophets. False prophets have lied by being allowed to tell the children (and, by inference, their parents) that happiness, fulfillment, and success will bring us joy. But the people discovered, perhaps too late, that those fake prophecies were wrong. So Jeremiah laments,

> The hearts of the people cry out to the Lord. You walls of Daughter Zion, let your tears flow like a river day and night; give yourself no relief, your eyes no rest. Arise, cry out in the night, as the watches of the night begin; pour out your heart like water in the presence of the Lord. Lift up your hands to him for the lives of your children, who faint from hunger at every street corner. (Lamentations 2:18–19 NIV)

It's a call to prayer. *Cry out from your heart!* He cries out, not unlike Paul Revere on his famous nighttime ride through a sleeping colony, "The enemy is attacking our children!"

The power of prayer may sound mundane or elementary, but don't underestimate what Jeremiah is saying. Take it as an imminent warning. The phrase *cry out* is multidimensional. It means to "shout"; it's an emotional plea. It speaks of someone who is serious. It means to "cry out for the children." It's passionate; it's raw; it's desperate. *Cry out to God* means to "yell" or "shout." And not because God is hard of hearing (He who speaks in a whisper is far from hard of hearing); it's yelling due to agitation, fear, and grave concern. Never underestimate the power of fervent prayer!

Have you ever been talking to someone and all of sudden they become agitated or incensed and their voice gets really loud? God says when you are praying about your children, don't roll over and lie down. *Take action!* These are your kids we're talking about. YOU HAVE TO MAKE YOUR VOICE HEARD! You can't just let the enemy come into your house and attack your children and think that your little patty-cake passive prayer is going to cut the mustard. No! You need to get down on your knees and look up to the Lamb of God and *cry out!*

Read Lamentations 2:18–19 again. Have you ever asked God to have mercy on your children? Maybe they were in bondage and oppression and you were seeing them suffer. Have you ever gone to God and cried out from your heart on behalf of your children that God would remove their suffering and struggles? It's a spirit that says, *I don't want to lose my child!* Or, if you don't have a child, whom are you standing in agreement with for a child in danger? Whose child do you know who's under attack? What family do you know that is being ravaged and shaken? *Cry out* literally means "holler." It's not a cool, sophisticated prayer with depth and nuance and layers and subliminal messages. It's guttural, it's raw, it's pleading, it's *sheer anxiety.*

One of the "mothers" in my home church—one of those saintly seniors who were prayer warriors and knew how to get a prayer through—could often be heard over the din of audible worship crying out with the eloquence of Ebonics: "Ham-mercy, Lawd! Ham-mercy!" It's the basest human emotion, crying out to our Maker for *HELP!* When your child, whom you helped raise and watched grow up, is under attack from the enemy, you have to cry out, "Have mercy on my child, Lord!"

The prophet says we need to *cry out,* to *shout to the Lord,* not for our stuff, but for our children. It's a prayer for intercession. It's a prayer for mediation. It's a prayer of mourning and grieving over the attacks of the enemy in your child's life. It speaks of the power and the posture of prayer. It means to stand in the gap.

Lamentations 2:19 says, "Arise, cry out in the night" (NIV). The phrase *in the night* means the time when folks should be asleep. It actually speaks of the first watch of the three watches of night. He says, "Get up and pray all night long. Wake up; don't sleep through the battle—get up! Pray, because it's dark, children." The book of John says the Messiah came into the world at a time when the people preferred darkness to light. That illuminates our problem today: we are praying for children of the night, children who live in a culture that prefers darkness.

This should be our sequence of response to the call:

1. *Wake up!* Remember, you're standing up in the darkness of the night watch, which makes the imperative even more urgent, because you can't always see what or who is around you.
2. *Stand up!* Jeremiah says, "Arise," which implies someone is sitting or lying down. Moreover, it implies that someone is not alert. It speaks of action.
3. *Speak up!* The prophet is telling us to cry out, speak up, "Lift up your hands to him for the lives of your children" (v. 19 NIV). We are to pray by the lifting of our hands.

Are you awake on behalf of someone's child who is suffering or struggling? Because God is saying to you, *wake up, stand up, and speak up* with uplifted hands in fervent prayer for that child.

You would want the same impassioned and urgent prayer response for your own child.

## CHAPTER 7

# FIGHT FOR THEM

*When David and his men saw the ruins and realized
what had happened to their families, they wept
until they could weep no more. . . . Then David asked the LORD,
"Should I chase after this band of raiders? Will I catch them?"
And the LORD told him, "Yes, go after them.
You will surely recover everything that was taken from you!"*

1 SAMUEL 30:3-4, 8 NLT

In the story above, David and his men had just returned from Aphek, where they had been with Achish (son of Maosh, king of Gath), preparing to help the Philistines go to battle against their enemies. At the last minute, after getting pushback from his men about letting David join in the looming war, Achish had sent David and his men back to Ziklag rather than allowing the Israelite to help the Philistines.

When they got back home, they discovered that the Amalekites had raided their town while they were gone, burned it to the ground, and carried off all women, children, and anyone else who was there. David and his men were devastated, but the Lord promised that they would get back everything—and every person—that had been stolen from them.

Knowing that in order to rescue everyone and recover everything, he was going to have to put up a fierce fight for them, David sought the Lord, asking Him one simple question: *Shall I chase them, and will I catch them?* Why didn't David just saddle up and grab his men and weapons and go get the Amalekites? After all, he was David, true king of Israel, the man who had killed his tens of thousands as the song went. The answer is that David wanted public confirmation that God was on his side, because he knew that if he failed, his men would kill him. Because they blamed him for the devastating loss of their families and possessions in the first place.

And God told him, *Go—you will bring back everything that was stolen.*

Before we look at the three lessons in this story, it's important to understand that not every theologian or Christian believes that God personally gives His input to someone who seeks His guidance or encouragement or help. However (and obviously), prayer would be pointless and the Holy Spirit wouldn't have much of a role to play in the Trinity if that were the case. Still, there are those who espouse a theological position known as *deism*, which denies the active involvement of God with His creation. So let's unpack this issue first.

It is believed that some of the founders of America were deists, men such as George Washington, Thomas Jefferson, and Alexander Hamilton. Other people believe that these men were actually Christians. Let me put that debate to rest: these men were *deists*. Period. They did not believe in the God of the Old and New Testaments.

Deism is the affirmation, the belief, the monotheistic position, that there is only one God. So far, so good. It is a position that sees God as transcendent; He created all that exists. Also sound theology. But then the deists add that after creating it all, God disengaged from His creation entirely. This is where you hear the needle scratching across the grooves of the record, because deists believe, essentially, that God went on a permanent cosmic vacation after His initial creation work was completed at the close of the sixth day. In other words, this position posits that God is still enjoying His seventh day of rest.

Some have nicknamed the deism theology as the "Watchmaker theory." At the risk of minimizing the theological complexities of this doctrine by oversimplifying the explanation of what deism is, I suggest that it is a concept of God that says He created the heavens and earth and then, like a watchmaker who has made a watch, God left His creation to tick away on its own, doing its job of telling time. In other words, once God made man and earth, He was done with it all. *Bye-bye. Good luck. See you later . . . maybe.*

Deism suggests that there is a God who created everything, but upon doing so He remained transcendent—awe-inspiring and magnificent—but He removed Himself and remains high above His creation, lofty yet no longer having any involvement or, presumably, any interest in what He made. Which, of course, would make prayer obsolete and unnecessary, and put all humanity at the mercy of the ravages of Satan and his henchmen.

The *McClintock and Strong Cyclopedia* gives some insight into deism:

> Deism focused on the glories of nature, especially human nature with its rational capacity. On the other hand, unlike Renaissance humanism it assigned God to the outer reaches of the universe, seeing him as only a beneficent, impersonal and artful creator. God was only marginally necessary. . . . Deism is the doctrine of God's relation to the world, which represents God as not only different, but also as separated from the world, therefore as only in an external relation to it; on the other hand, Theism would be the doctrine which represents God as holding an internal and real relation to the world.[1]

Deism emphasizes the transcendence of God and de-emphasizes the *imminence*—the proximity, the nearness of God. Put another way, deism says, "God is there, but He's not *here*." Deism is not atheism; deism does affirm there is a God. But He's just . . . out *there*, somewhere. He's not a God who is involved and engaged with His creation. Like a Great Observer in His skybox high above a coliseum, maybe occasionally glancing down at us in detached savoir faire as we scrape and duke it out far below in the arena of life.

Doesn't work that way. We're in this together. Because the biblical concept of God suggests that He is neither strictly transcendent nor solely imminent. He's *both*. He's transcendent *and* He's imminent. He is everywhere in time *and* at all times. He can be maddeningly distant and absent, and He can be wonderfully present and active. In fact, we humans, in all our soaring emotions and stoic strength, our indecision and steadfast focus, our tears and laughter and joy and anger . . . are living evidence that we were made *in His image*.[2] And His image is not one-dimensional; that is, He did not create, leave, stay away, and watch. He got involved with His creation. *Really* involved.

And He still is.

This preamble helps lay the foundation of the importance God places on family, and explains why, in 1 Samuel 30:3–4, David and his men felt bitter grief and wept until they could weep no more upon discovering that all of their family members had been captured by the Amalekites—and why our very involved God told David to go after them and guaranteed their success.

So, why does God place such high priority on family that He told David and his men to fight for them?

## THE BLESSING OF FAMILY

When God's first man, Adam, was done naming animals, God said, after observing and fellowshiping with Adam, "Man should not be alone." So, God created woman. This means that God recognized that there was no compatible helpmate for Adam. Which meant God was *involved* with Adam, observing him, assessing him. This God, then, who created the heavens and the earth, clearly and indisputably reveals Himself to be involved in His creation. So involved, in fact, that the very first time He expressed displeasure in creation was in reference to man lacking a friend, a soul mate to live life with. *Man should not be alone*—the thought of a highly engaged God.

So, our highly involved God gave Adam a wife, Eve, whom He made from a physical part of Adam's body. And then children came from Eve and Adam. And thus came the completion of the creation of the family unit (the first institution God created after creating man), which represents the continuity of the entire human race, which allows life to be passed on from generation to generation. Genealogy, then, is all about family. And family is one of the means God uses to communicate with humanity.

Family is the cosmic unit that is the central social context of human life. This first family, as dysfunctional as they were, formed a unit of companionship and relationship. Even in their dysfunction, the first family should give us hope, because our families today aren't much more messed up than was mankind's first family.

The book of Genesis gives us a first look at humanity's structured generations. Somebody begot somebody, who begot somebody, who begot somebody, and so forth; life from one generation to the next—the essence of continuity through family. This means that this God who created the heavens and the earth, then created man (the only creation that would interact and talk back to and with Him), then created woman, then created family, has continued to remain involved with His creation since the instance of the first creation and is still creating families.

Thus, God created family for three purposes: for companionship, for continuity, and for covenant. One very involved God.

## THE BLESSING OF COVENANT

God created and creates covenant in the context of family. Which means that the family is God's sovereign vehicle for making covenants. That is, He makes covenants always with the family in mind.

*Covenant* comes from a Hebrew word that means "to bind up." A covenant is a compact, a binding agreement, between two parties, that holds them to mutual undertakings on behalf of one another. Theologically used in relations between God and man, a covenant is initiated by God to denote a gracious undertaking entered into for the benefit of and blessing of mankind.

Covenants are specifically for those who by faith receive God's promises and commit themselves to the obligations that the undertaking involves. Even more than a contract, a covenant is administered like a partnership. That is, God, in His sovereignty, initiates a partnership that binds Him to a family and to mankind.

There are two shades of the meaning of *covenant* that are somewhat distinct to the Hebrew word for "covenant." One, in which it is more of a proper covenant voluntarily entered into, relates to a solemn mutual agreement. The other, in which it is more of a command than an obligation voluntarily assumed, is an obligation imposed by a superior upon a subordinate.

A *divine* covenant is one in which God agrees to fulfill unconditional promises made to people who truly trust Him.

Scripture reveals two types of covenants between God and mankind: first is the *unilateral divine covenant* such as the Abrahamic Covenant (see Genesis 12:1–3), which is unconditional and eternal, depending solely upon God for the ultimate fulfillment. The stipulation for enjoying the benefits of these unilateral divine covenants is one thing only: *obedient faith*. Second is the *mutual covenant* such as the Mosaic or Old Covenant, which requires both parties to fulfill certain conditions and obligations or else the agreement is broken. Thus, in a nutshell, the covenant involving God is a sovereignly administered relationship of union and communion between God and His people in the bonds of mutual faithfulness and love.

A one-sided covenant ("monopleuric") is one in which the covenant relation is purely an act of condescension or favor of God. Which means the covenant relation does not depend or wait upon the initiative of man. For example, the covenant through family is monopleuric (i.e., the biblical patriarch stories of God's blessings to families and descendants, generation after generation). Old Testament examples of monopleuric covenants are Abraham, Isaac, and Jacob, and the twelve tribes of Israel. New Testament examples of monopleuric covenants would be Lydia and the members of her household who were baptized.

A two-sided covenant ("dipleuric") is one that has man as a covenant partner with God. Because God has freely brought man into covenant with Himself, there are mutual obligations and conditions that devolve upon God with man within the covenant relation freely established and initiated by God.

The covenant, then, is the spoken blessing and favor of God. To bless people is to speak, to declare, the favor, the kindness, of God over their lives. The blessing must be transferred. God has chosen to transfer and to bestow covenant blessing in the context of the family from generation to generation. For example, in the Abrahamic Covenant, God said to Abraham, "I will bless you, and I will bless others through you." In other words, "I will make you into a great nation—and not just for you alone, but for others as well" (see Genesis 12:2). The covenant was passed to his son, Isaac. And then from Isaac to Jacob. And from Jacob to his twelve sons, who became twelve nations that blessed the world. Thus, the Abrahamic Covenant of *many who were blessed through one* was administered like a partnership because Abraham had a part to play: to initiate the passing of the blessing from one generation to the next.

## THE DEVIL'S COUNTERSTRATEGY

God's sovereign plan involving family prompted the devil's strategy. Satan quickly realized that the best strategy to break the transfer of the blessing chain was to attack the family so God's plan would be stopped. This was the devil's battle plan, which he executed in 1 Samuel 30. When David and his men returned home to Ziklag, they discovered that their city had been plundered, ravaged, torched down to the dirt. And their women and children had been kidnapped, preventing the perpetuation and creation of future generations. The devil's strategy was not just to take the city, but also to take out the next generation.

Upon realizing the horror that had taken place, David and his men wept so hard they couldn't even weep anymore. Have you ever cried over your child? Have you ever expected your child to be in one place, and when you saw that they weren't there, you wept? When you realize the cold emptiness where your children should have been but are not, you cry.

Then, as if David's own grief weren't enough, his men were grieving so hard they decided to kill *him*. Despair must have someone to blame, so, making things even worse, the men blamed their leader—even though he, too, was wrestling with the same emotions and anger and grief and pain at losing his family to the Amalekites. So now, in addition to wrestling with what's missing in his life, David is feeling guilty for what happened to their wives and children, because he was the leader and he had to have approved of leaving the women and children behind while he and his men went to fight alongside the Philistines, of all people—avowed longtime enemies of the Israelites. Talk about a guilt trip.

Have you ever questioned yourself for actions or decisions you've taken in your life?

*What did I do wrong?*

*Did I drop the ball there?*

*Was it that they didn't receive the blessing, or did I somehow fail to pass the blessing on to them?*

*What do I do now?*

Have you ever felt guilty and didn't really know exactly what you had done to feel guilty about, or if it was even your fault? Welcome to David's dilemma when he arrived home at Ziklag. *What did I do wrong? And how do I fix it?*

## OUR BATTLE STRATEGY

So, what does David do next? He encourages himself. Sometimes the only encouragement you can get is from yourself. Maybe your close friend is not answering the phone. You try to call your pastor, but the answering machine says he's not available. You call the prayer hotline, and they put you on hold! Like David, sometimes you just have to encourage yourself. Donald Lawrence captured this truth in his song "Encourage Yourself," recorded with the contemporary gospel group the Tri-City Singers:

> *The enemy created walls, but remember giants, they do fall;*
> *speak over yourself, encourage yourself in the Lord.*[3]

David didn't get encouragement from his men for two reasons: first, the men were grieving over their loss; and second, the men were angrily blaming David for their loss and were thinking about putting him to the sword for it.

Obviously, his men weren't serious about actually committing the ultimate act of treason by killing their leader, the true king of Israel (even though Saul refused to stand down), king of Judah. But his men were displeased with him enough to talk about it. Have you ever been so disappointed by someone's actions, so angry at the results of their mistake, that you said something like, "Man, I am so ticked off at him I want kill him!" You know you're not plotting murder; it's just a colloquial expression of livid frustration. That may have been the state of mind behind these soldiers' anger, but if they truly were mad enough to kill him, the second book of Kings would have ended abruptly and the rest of the Old Testament would have flowed quite differently.

Sometimes you will go through tough experiences and folk who want to help you won't or can't. So you have to learn how to find something, some substance, some grit, an anchor deep down inside you to encourage yourself. You have to go to that person in the mirror and say, "This is going to be a rough day, but you're going to come through this! You may have made some mistakes, but you're going to get to the other side of this! It's not over yet!" You have to pat yourself on the back, encourage yourself, and remind yourself who you are and what kind of God you serve.

There will be times when the devil will make you think you haven't done anything right. Those are the times when you need to remind yourself of some of the sacrifices you made, how you've wept for your child, how you went above and beyond, and see for yourself that you haven't done all that bad. So give yourself a standing ovation. Accept your own applause. Sometimes you have to encourage yourself.

But with David, it didn't stop there. The next verse says he goes to God. In the midst of his anger and grief, 1 Samuel 30:6 says he "found strength in the LORD his God" (NIV). I think that's the key: you encourage yourself by going to God! Never find comfort that is not confirmed by God. That is, don't make yourself comfortable in unconfirmed comfort.

David encourages himself; then he goes to the Lord and asks, "Shall I pursue this raiding party? Will I overtake them?" (v. 8). God answers, "Pursue them" (v. 8 NIV). "You will surely recover everything that was taken from you" (NLT).

There's a danger when we comfort ourselves with a "comfort zone" that contradicts the Word of God. Someone might argue, "But it's less expensive for two to live together than separately." Well, that may be a comforting idea, but if it's not confirmed by the Word of God, then you're opening the door to a scheme of the devil. Because it's a trick of the enemy to allow yourself to get comfortable in a lifestyle that contradicts the Word of God. Sure, you can find a level of fleshly, material, financial, or convenience comfort outside the will of God, but the generational example set by David was to first encourage himself and then get confirmation from God. *Lord, should I go after them—and will I succeed?* He was taking no chances, not after the disaster that had awaited them when they'd returned to Ziklag.

This brings us to three lessons behind David's battle strategy for going after the Amalekites to rescue his and his men's family members and recover their belongings.

## THREE LESSONS FROM
## DAVID'S BATTLE STRATEGY

Our tendency is to talk ourselves into comfort and then rationalize our position. But if our rationalized position is outside of the will of God, it is still unconfirmed and is a setup to a letdown. Here was David's three-prong battle strategy after first getting confirmation from God to go after the Amalekites:

1. Go and overtake the enemy.
2. Defeat the enemy.
3. Bring the women, children, and possessions back home.

The Lord said, "Go in." So they went in, fought and won, and brought back everything the enemy had taken from them. You cannot win the battle unless you go to the battlefield. The deception of the saints is that they think the battle is fought when they're in church. As long as the saints go to church every seventh day, they think they're going to war. Consider the songs we sing in the church:

"I'm a Soldier in the Army of the Lord."

"I'm on the Battlefield for My Lord."

"Onward, Christian Soldiers."

If you're such a soldier in the army of the Lord, then why do you get upset when the enemy takes shots at you? The first thing you must do is go into the enemy's camp (which means you must learn where his camp is). And second, you must *fight*.

David and his men went in, caught the enemy off guard, the battle ensued, and David gained the victory.

Imagine the Amalekites after escaping with David's and his men's possessions and property and women and children: they're divvying up the spoils, choosing wives from among the bedraggled women they had kidnapped and force marched to the Amalekite stronghold, and are deciding which of the frightened children they will use as their own slaves. The Amalekite soldiers are chortling in the realization that they just pulled a fast one on the famous, mighty David, true king of Israel, son of Jesse the

Bethlehemite, and got away with ripping off all he had left behind when he went up to Aphek to do battle against the enemies of the Philistines. The Amalekites are partying and whooping it up when some of them feel an ever-so-faint tremor in the ground . . . like the distant pounding of horse hooves. They stop their festivities . . . they look all around them, all the way to the horizon and the setting orange sun . . . they listen hard . . . they hear a racket from afar . . . and they figure it's probably the reverberations of their own partying echoing off of the rocky hillsides. So they resume their revelry and debauchery with their victims.

Suddenly at dusk, four hundred men led by David come thundering into the Amalekite camp with righteous fury and indignation, adrenaline gushing through their systems, swords swinging, spears thrusting. After a fierce battle that lasts all the way from sundown and into the evening of the next day, the Amalekites are cut down by the vengeance of the followers of Almighty Jehovah.

"Four hundred Amalekites rode away on camels, but they were the only ones who escaped," the Bible says (1 Samuel 30:17 CEV). Which implies that David's four-hundred-man force had defeated an army far bigger than his. David's men knew that if they were to bring back the next generation, they had to fight for them. And the fight was worth it. They recovered everything. Not a woman or child, not a gold ring or donkey was lost.

You may have lost some battles in your life, but you've got to let the devil know that even though you're exhausted, heartbroken, weary, and numb, you will fight another round. Encourage yourself in the Lord. Fret not yourself against evildoers, for soon they will be cut down. Remind yourself, "I stand with enough fight in me, knowing that greater is He who is in me than he who is in the world. I stand for battle, because I can do all things through Christ, who strengthens me."

Your son, your daughter, your grandchild, your legacy, your family are worth the fight. You've had struggles and battles, but you would never leave your child wounded at the hands of the enemy. Sometimes, as tired as you are, you have to tell the devil, "I still have some fight in me, so take your best shot, because I am encouraged in the Lord!"

Fight—for *them*.

## CHAPTER 8

# GO TO
# WAR

*For we wrestle not against flesh and blood,*
*but against principalities, against powers, against the rulers*
*of the darkness of this world, against spiritual wickedness*
*in high places. . . . And take the helmet of salvation,*
*and the sword of the Spirit, which is the word of God.*

EPHESIANS 6:12, 17 KJV

In 1970, a cultural prophet of sorts spoke out against the myriad challenges that faced America at the dawn of a new decade in America. Nixon was in the White House. The nation was not yet healed from the violence of the 1968 Republican primary convention. Vietnam was still raging out of control, with America doing what it had been doing there for decades, with the president denying it all, same as previous presidents before him.

But change was coming.

This cultural prophet was named Edwin Starr, and he was a Motown troubadour of song. He was no Marvin Gaye or Curtis Mayfield, but the brother could sing. He spoke out in an antiwar protest song that was one of the first Motown songs to make a political statement. Written by Norman Whitfield and Barrett Strong, the song was originally recorded by the Temptations in 1969, the same summer I graduated from the University of Illinois. It caught my ear and became part of a sometimes-silent mantra of mine when I joined the Marine Corps. The premise of the song suggested that people did not fully understand what war was good for, and sought to educate the world on that topic through musical sociopolitical commentary against the war in Vietnam. I thought it was a cool song with a catchy, syncopated beat, but the Temptations' version of the tune languished on the charts and never really gained popularity. That is, until Edwin Starr's rendition of the song hit the airwaves in the summer of 1970 like a rifle butt to the head.

The song was titled "War," and it posed a simple question:

"War: What is it good for?" Which was followed by the stark reply, "Absolutely *nothin'*!" Starr sang the song in an angry and dramatic soul shout that attacked the question and answer with the clamor and energy of a wrecking ball on a corner liquor store. He slammed out the song's premise that if people didn't fully get the purpose of war—Vietnam in particular, at the time—then here's what war was good for: *absolutely nothing!* The song transported the listener from the battlefields and rice paddies of Vietnam to the broken homes and shattered families of the brave warriors of that evil war and, in the end, personalized it. Starr's loud, raging vocals assumed that those who supported the war in 'Nam did not understand the seriousness and violent finality of war, and he was there to teach them about it in less than four minutes. And did he ever.

I was in the Marine Corps Reserve at the time, having completed my six months of boot camp as a Marine recruit in San Diego. For five and a half years I would return to my local base one weekend every month, plus two weeks each summer, to perform my duty. I made several friends in boot camp; one, whom we will call Raythel McKinny, hailed from Mississippi. During our downtimes, we Marines would often hear Raythel, his lanky body slung over his cot, singing along to "War" as it blared out of a little transistor radio with a tinny speaker, his voice cracking and slightly off-key, his eyes focused, his heart full.

The song became an instant smash hit around the world, earning a Grammy nomination the following year. It would go on to be covered by artists the likes of Bruce Springsteen, featured in movies such as Jackie Chan's *Rush Hour*, and played on television shows like *The Simpsons*. Throughout the ensuing decades, it would be covered by countless other singers and artists and bands.

Raythell McKinny died in Vietnam. The war took him in his prime, amid the echoes of a sociocultural prophet named Edwin Starr, who wanted to educate the world about the essence of war. A lesson Raythel learned all too violently and far too young.

## THE REAL WAR

Possibly the most effective strategy of the devil is to deceive nations, peoples, and cultures as to his very existence. Nineteenth-century French author, poet, translator, writer, and art critic Charles Baudelaire, in his 1864 short story "The Generous Gambler," eloquently made this point when he wrote, "la plus belle des ruses du diable est de vous persuader qu'il n'existe pas!" (*the loveliest trick of the devil is to persuade you he does not exist!*).[1]
In truth, the devil warrants little or no attention, but the uninitiated and the unsaved take it too far by categorizing him as myth—and that is Satan's most effective weapon in convincing people not to worry about him or to pay any heed to what he's up to as he goes to and fro in the earth. After all, if he "doesn't exist" to many people, then he's free to run rampant and wreak havoc in their lives.

The devil's successful strategy to remove from the mind-set of society any consideration of an evil supernatural force is an integral factor in the lives of millions of his innocent victims. Even within much of the church, there has been a tendency to minimize the efforts of (and in some cases, the very existence of) Satan and his demonic host. This thinking has hindered the church's effectiveness in reaching the world for Christ, and continues to water down the gospel. The Motown song should have cried out, "Devil: What is he there for? To leave you *absolutely nothin'*!"

The essence of the Christian life is knowing that the ultimate victory over Satan and evil has already been won by Christ through His death and resurrection, yet the church must not let down its guard in the daily (yea, hourly) battle of defending God's kingdom here on earth until Christ returns to claim it. As I quoted at the top of this chapter, Ephesians 6:12 reminds us that our real fight is not against flesh and blood, not against people here on earth, not against enemies we can see. The real battle is against the enemy we can't see—Satan and his cadre of evil and the spiritual wickedness warring in the heavens.

Spiritual warfare has its origin in a rebellion of many angels against God, led by the former Lucifer (Satan, as this ex-chief cherubic angel was called after his ejection from heaven), who leads an army of forces opposed to God. Several scriptures highlight his power in the earth. In John 12:31 and 14:30, Satan is referred to by Jesus as the prince of *this* world, not of the spirit world. In Ephesians 2:2, Satan is referred to as the "prince of the power of the air" (KJV) or, in another version, as the "ruler of the kingdom of the air" (NIV), which speaks to how he exercises influence globally and within each culture in this world. Satan is alive and he is on a mission. In Job 1:7 he is going "to and fro in the earth" (KJV). In 1 Peter 5:8, the devil is our enemy who "prowls around like a roaring lion" (NIV) "seeking whom he may devour" (KJV).

It is a sad truth that very few Christians have understood the insidious yet overt battle we are in today. Very few have taken a strong and courageous stand against the worldly spirit of this age as it destroys our culture and the Christian ethos that once helped shape our country. But the Scriptures make clear that we, as Bible-believing Christians, are locked in a vicious war of cosmic proportions, a life-or-death struggle for the minds and souls of each generation over all the earth.

The devil is devious, deceptive, and he has a very simple agenda: to short-circuit and destroy the plan of God in our lives. If we are going to pass generational blessings, it would be foolish not to assume that the passing of these blessings becomes a target of the enemy. Our spiritual heads are in the metaphorical sand if we assume the devil is not interested in what is passed from one generation to the next. And he's getting better at his job of stealing, killing, and destroying in each successive generation.

My last name is Ulmer, the name of my father's ancestors. The name originated from the city of Ulm, in Germany. I assume the name came from the slave owners of my ancestors in Ulm. I have no blood brothers. I am the last Ulmer in the bloodline of my daddy. Now, if my children don't pass that name, that name will die. It is the blocking and stopping of passing from one generation to the next that catches the attention of the enemy. If he can potentially stop blessings from flowing from one generation to the next, then he can stop the blessing on the entire family permanently. And if he can do that in every family (and trust me, he's trying), that would be the end. Indeed, it has been argued that Christianity could be just one generation away from extinction.

There is a war going on in the world. Certainly we see it bubbling violently to the surface in far-flung places like Syria and

Afghanistan and Israel and Gaza and Iraq and on and on around the world. We also see the effects in our cities here at home, in Chicago and St. Louis and Charlottesville and New York and Las Vegas and Newtown and Columbine and Los Angeles; the American list is endless. But it's the spiritual war that would rob each generation of the blessings, the teachings, the lessons, the earned collective wisdom of the previous generation. And the enemy's goal is to have you either altogether dismiss the spiritual connection of the war going on or not be aware of it at all.

This world either secularizes, humanizes, or denies the very existence of Satan. The agnostic, atheistic thread running through culture that denies God, by definition, also denies demons and Satan and evil powers that work behind the scenes. But we cannot believe in God and *not* believe in Satan, or believe in heaven and *not* believe in hell, any more than we can believe the sun doesn't shine in Phoenix or Riyadh at noontime in the dead of summer. You have to know that you are in a war, despite today's culture overtly opposing that truth.

The late Walter Hawkins prophetically proclaimed the reality of this war in his song "There's a War Going On," which was based on Paul's Ephesians revelation. He sang about why we need the armor of the Lord:

> *There's a war going on and if you're gonna win*
> *You better make sure that you have Jesus deep down*
> *within.*

There indeed is a war going on; statistics bear it out. In my earlier drafts of this work, I cited a series of statistics about the family, the breakdown of the family, the rising number of children being raised in single-parent homes, the relationship between children raised in fatherless homes and crime, and statistics on the relationship between poverty, drug use, and suicide among those raised in fatherless homes, as well as the number of teenage pregnancies across America today. The numbers were pretty discouraging.

The more I read and reread the passage, I decided not to include those statistics in this book. To tell the truth, they depressed me and pained me with an overwhelming sense of helplessness, frustration, and cynicism. I think the statistic that gripped me most was the revelation and affirmation of a growing sociological suspicion that churches no longer hold the appeal for our young people as they did in the past. As a result, churches are closing their doors at a shocking rate, with approximately eight to ten thousand houses of worship permanently shutting their doors each year.[2]

I trace these discouraging realities to a satanic source. By no means am I attempting to extract the human element of cognitive choices and willful demonstrations of the desire and determination of people to live their own lives as they please. But I suggest that the trail to the source of such a mind-set leads to the powers of darkness and spiritual wickedness in high places. I suggest that such a mind-set can even open the door to self-proclaimed Christians believing that people who merely claim the mantle of Christianity while consistently evincing no actions or words or attitudes or ways we Christians are to display are nevertheless fellow Christians and should be given a pass for the lack of evidence of Christianity in their lives. But Matthew 7:16 reminds us that we will know our fellow Christians by the way they live their lives: "By their fruit you will recognize them" (NIV).

The enemy simply does not want you to believe he exists, and he will do and say anything to keep you in that state of ignorance. Because the instant you realize that it is absolute, logical, factual truth that he is at work against you, he knows he's on his way to losing his battle to take you down.

## WHERE WAR RESIDES

When Apostle Paul pointed out in 2 Corinthians the truth established by God, "though we walk in the flesh, we do not war after the flesh" (10:3 KJV), he wasn't referring to "flesh" in the sense of sin. He was talking about flesh in the sense of humanity, our humanness, *people.* We walk in the flesh, but the real war is not in the flesh. The assumption is that we are in a war, but we do not really war in the sphere of the flesh (that's only one end result of the war we are engaged in against the rulers of the realm of spiritual wickedness).

As Paul states in Ephesians 6:12 at the beginning of this chapter, Christians *wrestle not.* Another version says we *"struggle" not* (NIV). The point Paul is making is that we Christians don't wrestle in the way you might think—that is, in the physical, face-to-face world. There is a deeper, more insidious war going on. We Christians wrestle another way, the spiritual battle way, against "demonic" spirit operatives working from the dark side, the devil's side. It is a war in the spirit realm. This wrestling match, this inside war, is being waged for control of our belief, our thought process, our way of life.

The real battlefield is in the heavenlies, in the high places. I'm not going to wander out of my lane to chase a rabbit trail into the deep and profound exegesis of heaven. But I will assume, from a biblical study on the topic, that there is more than one celestial sphere or location known as "heaven." In fact, the Bible speaks of three heavens. Genesis 1:1 says God created "the heavens" (plural) and the earth (NIV). I suggest this heaven may refer to the atmosphere surrounding the earth. Exodus 32:13 speaks of the "stars of heaven" (KJV), referring to what I believe is commonly spoken of as "outer space." The stars, sun, and moon are beyond our atmosphere, but they exist in the span of planets and heavenly objects. In 2 Corinthians 12:1–4, Paul goes beyond that space and speaks of "paradise" (NIV), stating that he was once transferred to that space. The word he uses for *paradise* is the same word for *garden* (as in the Garden of Eden), a place of magnificence.

Some say the first heaven is where the birds fly and the second heaven is where the planets and sun and moon exist in perpetual orbit. As one online Bible study explains, "This celestial location is the atmosphere that surrounds the earth, the place where clouds exist and birds, along with jets, fly in every day. Jeremiah confirms where this place is located in the fourth chapter and verse 25. The place where airplanes and birds fly in we call SKY. The book of Revelation [19:17] states this fact when it says, '. . . birds that fly in the midst of HEAVEN.'"[3]

Paul strains to help us understand his supernatural, otherworldly experience by suggesting that the third heaven is the dwelling place of God: "I knew a man in Christ above fourteen years ago, (whether in the body, I cannot tell; or whether out of the body, I cannot tell: God knoweth;) such an one caught up to the third heaven" (2 Corinthians 12:2 KJV).

So, the first heaven is the atmosphere surrounding earth. The second heaven is what we might call "outer space" or stellar heavens of stars and planets—this is the realm in which angels operate (in Job 38:7, angels are called *stars*—"when the morning stars sang together" [KJV]), and the third heaven is the throne room of God in heaven (the "control center" of His universe, so to speak).

Not to go too deep into the theological discussion, but to try to simplify the discussion a bit more, there certainly are at least two *realms*: the unseen spirit realm and the materialistic, perceptible earthly realm. The "heavenlies" is the spiritual sphere where God, Christ, the spiritual powers, and believers exist together. (Our five senses are not the limit of reality; everything we see in the visible, physical realm is caused, provoked, or at least influenced by something in the invisible spiritual realms.) Believers live both in the physical world and at the same time are seated with the risen Christ in the heavenlies, where they are enjoying their spiritual blessings *while also* being engaged in the real battle—the battle for their souls against the demonic powers here on earth.

If you are engaged in a spiritual battle and need help, that help must come from the heavenly place, from the spirit realm where the battle occurs. Ephesians 2:6 says we are seated in the heavenly places at the right hand of the Father with Christ the Son. So we are in the heavenly places. When you accepted Christ, you were transported to another atmosphere. Even though your body is limited to the dimension of earth, your spirit (which should be controlling your body) is operating in a different realm.

In Ephesians 6:12, Paul used governmental terms lifted from the Roman world to articulate the organization of demonic forces that do Satan's bidding. He listed the rankings of the demonic world, which is comprised of Satan's fellow fallen angels. These territorial demons control people and even entire nations.

We now have a vertical view of the war in which we're fighting. We walk on low ground, but we war in high places. We walk in the earthly realm, but we war in the spirit realm. Therefore, if you spend any time warring against anything wrapped in flesh and blood, *you are fighting the wrong enemy!* It's never about *him* or *her.* If you ever get your focus off the real battle and onto him or her, you're in the wrong battle, because they are wrapped in flesh and blood. Therefore they are not the real enemy. And if you are engaging in battle with them, you are stopping your own spiritual progress—which is the very thing the devil wants.

Wrestling against flesh and blood is a strategy of the enemy. The devil wants you to stay away from resisting him in the true theater of war. He wants you to waste time bickering and squabbling with people and fighting against your fellow human beings. Because he knows if he can get you fighting the wrong enemy on the wrong battlefield, you'll lose the real battle completely. In fact, you never even showed up; you lost by default.

There is a kind of legend in my hometown. One time in East St. Louis, there was a football game between my school, East St. Louis Senior High (East Side), and Belleville High from the city "up the hill" from us. In our conference, most of the sports teams had their own fields. Other teams, like ours, had a community field that was shared by different sports teams. When Belleville arrived, they went to the wrong field. We waited for them at the right field. They waited for us at the wrong field. And they lost the game by forfeit, because they played a waiting game on the wrong field.

Likewise, the devil wants you to get stuck on the wrong battlefield and lose by forfeit because you don't show up where the real battle occurs.

My friend Dr. Tony Evans, who has a brilliant mind, has probably the best definition I've ever heard about what spiritual warfare truly is: spiritual warfare is conflict being waged in the invisible, spiritual realm that is being manifested in the visible, physical realm and affects you and me. The cause is ultimately related to the war between God and Satan, but we can only see the effects in the natural. Good Dr. Evans says:

> Until you recognize that your struggle is not with man but with spiritual hosts of wickedness in the heavenly places, you will never begin to live in victory. Your victory in spiritual warfare must rest on the reality that God has given you everything that you need to live in light of the truth of His victory in order to experience and become all that God has created you to be. But God will not dress you in the weapons of warfare.[4]

Apostle Paul wants us to know we fight a certain battle against a certain enemy on a certain battleground, and that none of that fight takes place in the earth realm, because if you're in a fight in the earth realm, you didn't do your prep work for the battle in the spirit realm, and you are doomed to be trounced.

The origin of the battle is between light and darkness, between God and the devil. God's foot soldiers are called angels. The devil's foot soldiers are called principalities, powers, rulers of darkness (which are, in essence, a hierarchy of demonism). They are under the command of the don, the mafia boss, the devil himself, Satan. (Dr. Evans calls demons the devil's "spiritual mafia"; they move on his orders against the people of God.)

Ultimately, the battle is some manifestation of a longtime strategy of Satan to get back at God for ejecting him from heaven for the sin of pride. Yet, the manifestation of that battle is down here on earth. At the end of the day, it's not about us; we're just caught in the crossfire of the war Satan started against God. We're just the devil's pawns in this battle in the spirit realm that we can't see but which impacts our prayer life, our faith, and our daily walk with the Lord.

One of the favorite battles of the enemy is over and in the family. In this war, the enemy gets the victory when husbands bicker with their wives, when parents fight against their children, and one generation turns against another in unresolved conflicts. All of these fights take place in the physical earth realm, which means family is on its way to defeat, because the real battle already took place—on the spiritual battlefield, where there is no wrestling against flesh and blood. In essence, a family defeats itself like a circular firing squad or by "friendly fire" when they take the devil's bait and bicker among themselves.

The believer has three enemies: the world, the flesh, and the devil. One of the great influences in my ministerial life was

Dr. David Hocking, a professor at Grace Graduate School of Theology. (I was impressed by the brilliant theologian because he was the first person I had met who had earned two doctorates—a doctor of ministry and a doctor of philosophy—and academically, I wanted to be just like him.) One of the many things that Dr. Hocking indelibly imprinted into my life was the revelation of the three enemies of the believer and their goals—the world, the flesh, and the devil:

1. The world wants to give you success without God.
2. The flesh wants to give you pleasure without God.
3. And the devil wants to make you religious without God.

Let that sink in for a minute. It's a simple yet *profound* truth.

Dr. Ray Stedman, a contemporary of Dr. Hocking, further clarified the battle we face. Dr. Stedman said that "there is not three. There is only one enemy, the devil, as Paul brings out in Ephesians 6. But the channels of his indirect approach to men are through the world and the flesh."[5] Dr. Stedman continues:

The flesh in this context, is not our bodies, not the meat and blood and bones of our physical life. [Flesh] is a term which describes the urge to self-centeredness within us, that distortion of human nature which makes us want to be our own god—that proud ego, that uncrucified self which is the seat of willful defiance and rebellion against authority. . . . The world, on the other hand, is the corporate expression of all the flesh-centered individuals who make up the human race. Since the flesh is in every one of them—acting satanic, devilish, sensual, earthly—the total combined expression of such beings constitutes the world and determines the philosophy of the world.[6]

In other words, the strategy of the devil is to distract us from the real war and distort the identity of the true enemy: Satan himself. To that, Dr. Stedman adds, "Most often the devil comes in disguise, through the channel of the flesh . . . that is what the apostle warns against when he speaks of the 'wiles of the devil.'"[7] Again, the most common trick and trap of the enemy is to get us fighting the wrong enemy: anyone in flesh and blood. If we are fighting and the enemy is wrapped in flesh and blood, he's *gotcha!* You're fighting the wrong enemy, because remember, as Paul says in Ephesians 6:12, "our struggle is not against flesh and blood" (NIV).

When Ephesians 6:12 says that we "we wrestle [struggle] not against flesh and blood, but against principalities, against powers, against the rulers of the darkness of this world, against spiritual wickedness in high places [the hierarchy of the enemy]" (KJV), the key is the word *wrestle*, which means "hand-to-hand combat." This word is used as in a wrestling match, where you have to get your hands on your opponent and rough them up and gain control over them. Paul is saying, *Here's what the war looks like, folks: hand-to-hand combat.*

As I mentioned earlier, Edwin Starr's world-famous 1970 rendition of the counterculture-era soul song "War" was featured in the Jackie Chan movie *Rush Hour.* In one pivotal scene, upon hearing this song, rather than risk looking foolish trying to join in the dance steps of his costar Chris Tucker, Chan's character interprets Tucker's dance moves with a series of karate hand movements, as a metaphor for hand-to-hand combat. While Tucker is dancing and singing about the war, Chan is getting into position with his karate hand movements as the anti-war song plays.[8]

Ours is not the type of war where you push a button from the other side of the world, sending a missile from one place to another, or launching an armed drone to wreak havoc in another nation. Our war in the spirit is like hand-to-hand combat, which implies a personal, intimate war. It's a war that impacts your entire life and your daily journey here on earth.

Welcome to the war.

## OUR RESOURCES FOR WAR

Paul employs several metaphors in 2 Corinthians 10:3–6 to reinforce the point that a war is going on:

- War is being waged (10:3).
- Weapons of warfare are used to destroy strongholds (v. 4).
- Obstacles against God are torn down (v. 5).
- Captives are taken (v. 5).
- Rebels will be punished (v. 6).

I suggest that this war, which is intimate and hand to hand, is on the turf of the most precious values and relationships in our lives. It is not about our surface, transient, superfluous fly-by-night encounters and involvements. It is a battle on the intimate foundational priorities by which we define and defend our very essence. This includes our relationship with God and our intimate relationships with our family and loved ones.

Adam and Eve revealed relationship as the priority of creation: the first relationship was between God and Adam, and the second was between Adam and Eve. This is the family God established and from which all future generations flowed. Since the war against Satan and his battle against family are up close and personal, God has given us spiritual weapons, resources, armor, and defenses to use in the war (as it says in 2 Corinthians 10:4, "For the weapons of our warfare are not carnal, but mighty through God to the pulling down of strong holds" [KJV]).

Stand firm then, with the belt of truth buckled around your waist, with the breastplate of righteousness in place, and with your feet fitted with the readiness that comes from the gospel of peace. In addition to all this, take up the shield of faith, with which you can extinguish all the flaming arrows of the evil one. Take the helmet of salvation and the sword of the Spirit, which is the word of God. (Ephesians 6:14–17 NIV)

In the passage above, Paul lists every piece of armor we have at our disposal that is used for defense:

- The belt of truth around our waist secures our uniform.
- The breastplate of righteousness in place protects our heart and organs.
- Our feet standing firm protects our balance and stability.

- The shield of faith extinguishes the flaming arrows of the devil.

And finally, the only combination offensive/defensive weapons we have:

- The helmet of salvation protects our mind, our thinking, our eternal security.
- The sword of the Spirit is the Word of God.

As Fritz Rienecker writes in *Linguistic Key to the Greek New Testament*, these weapons are "instruments of warfare, a general word used for both defensive and offensive weapons."[9] While Paul uses the phrase "the weapons of our warfare," we only have one actual weapon. Everything else is gear for our protection. The one true weapon we have is the sword of the Spirit, which is the Word of God.

There are two words for *sword*, one of which is a sword with a long blade, with which one fights at a distance. But the word used in Ephesians 6:17 for *sword* does not refer to a long sword; it refers to what is more like a dagger or a big knife. It's right at hand, in your belt, used for "intimate" close-up battle, hand-to-hand combat. With the short sword, you're able to respond quickly, in short, quick thrusts and slashes.

Paul says the weapons we have are not of this world but are empowered by the Spirit, who activates this particular type of sword of the Spirit as a weapon when utilized and handled in the Spirit—which is the Word of God. This is the one wieldable weapon we have for offensive measures. Every other weapon is for defense. After you've done everything else possible to prevail, once you take up this offensive weapon, the sword of the Spirit, you can stand, because you're covered in protection.

You would think Paul would have said, "After you've done all you can, *attack!*" So, why would he say to "stand"? Because we stand in order to protect what we've already been given by God. He is saying, *If you just stand in place, after you've done everything you can to stand, keep on standing in position.* The victory has already been given as long as you hang on. You will be victorious as long as you *stay in the battle.* Stand, and see the salvation of the Lord. To be victorious, all you have to do is *hang in there.* Don't give up, don't throw in the towel.

The key to the "sword of the Spirit/Word of God" weapon is in the phrase *the Word.* The most common word for the phrase *the Word of God* is "logos" (we would call it the Bible). It speaks of the Word in totality. It speaks of the body and entirety of the Word God delivered. However, when the Bible speaks of your weapon being the Word of God, it is not speaking of the Word in totality, of Genesis to Revelation. When you're in the midst of a battle, Genesis to Revelation won't help you. To understand the true, kinetic power of God's Word, you have to see the Word (Genesis to Revelation) as a *scabbard,* a sheath, that holds the blade—which is the sword/word, the offensive spiritual weapon that does the cutting. In other words, you have to be able to pull a word out of the Word.

In a somewhat obscure work on the book of Ephesians, Ruth Paxson, a missionary in China, explained it like this:

The word of God was the one weapon used by Jesus in the wilderness when, as the Representative Man, He won not only His victory, but ours too, over the devil. Each of Satan's three attacks was met with a sword of the Spirit, "It is written," and three times Satan was repulsed. Only as we use this mighty weapon with intelligence and skill will we be able to withstand Satan successfully. This will require of us a constant, systematic study of God's word, that our sword may be easily and quickly unsheathed, and that just the needed part of it may be used at the right time and in the right way.[10]

In the New Testament "the word of God" is never a general reference to "Holy Scriptures"; it's a word God gives us *to speak*. To be able do this at any time—and particularly in the midst of battle—we must be rooted in Scripture, because Scripture is the primary source of God's word. Paul's suggestion is that the Christian may be open to, and can always depend on, receiving the needed word from the Word of God. But the challenge in that suggestion is that we need to be equipped with sufficient knowledge of the Word to wield that blade—that *rhema* word utterance—as a weapon at the ready. It may be a word of comfort for one's emotional turmoil, a word of hope for one's anxious mind, a word of condemnation for one's sin, a word of prophetic judgment for one's disengagement or insensitivity. It may also be the word a Christian is to speak, a witness to be uttered, a teaching to be shared. It is the word of the Bible made alive by the Spirit for our edification and for our witness, admonition, and exhortation with others. It is also the inbreaking of God by His Spirit speaking to our spirit, and through our spirit to others.

Look at it like this: somewhere in the Word, between Genesis and Revelation, there is a *word* for your victory in the battle you're in. But when you go to battle, you don't take a time-out to go through Genesis to Revelation. In battle, you've got to be able to pull a word out of the Word immediately, to cover the situation effectively. And that word you pull out is a *rhema* word (not *logos*, which is the Bible in its entirety), an utterance, a spiritual-word weapon at the ready.

As an imagined example, the Spirit sword of the Word battle between Jesus and Satan in Matthew 4 might look something like this:

SATAN (coy, imperious): "If thou be the Son of God, command that these stones be made bread" (v. 3 KJV).

JESUS (fierce, unmoving): "It is written" (v. 4 KJV)— *WHOOSH*—swings the sword of Deuteronomy 8:3, "Man shall not live by bread alone, but by every word that proceedeth out of the mouth of God" (v. 4 KJV)!

SATAN (knocked all the way back to the holy city, wounded from the blow and breathing hard as he perches on the very pinnacle of the Temple): "Okay, okay! Then if Thou *really* be the Son of God, as You claim, then cast Thyself down—*for it is written*"—*SHWING*— lashes back with Psalm 91:11–12, "He shall give his angels charge concerning thee! And in their hands they shall bear thee up, lest at any time thou dash thy foot against a stone!" (vv. 5–6 KJV).

JESUS (moving in for the kill, sword raised): "It is written, again" —*ZANG*—stabs at Satan with Deuteronomy 6:16, "Thou shalt not tempt the Lord thy God" (v. 7 KJV)!

SATAN (bleeding, giving up on the Word and letting his sword clatter to the ground as he flees to an exceeding high mountain, where he waves an arm indicating all the kingdoms of the world and stutters, eyes wild with fright as he faces off with his very Maker): "Wait, *wait!*—all these things will I give Thee! If, if Thou wilt—just someday, doesn't have to be right now!—but someday just, you know, fall down and worship me!" (vv. 8–9 KJV).

JESUS (victorious, raising His sword, looking down at the groveling beast): "Get thee hence, you sniveling little wimp, for it is written"—*SWISH*—back-swings at Satan's fleeing rear with Deuteronomy 6:13, "Thou shalt worship the Lord thy God! And Him only shalt thou serve!" (v. 10 KJV).

SATAN (scurries away in search of more certain prey—hopefully one who hasn't such a solid grasp of the sword of the Word at hand—of which he knows there are plenty in the world . . . even self-admitted followers of this crafty Jesus fellow.)

As this imagined scene of that famous Matthew 4:3–11 encounter displays, we must be ready to draw on specific truths from the Bible during specific temptations and attacks from the enemy. It is the word in your hand and in your heart that brings victory. The person filled and controlled by the Holy Spirit knows how to handle the sword in specific spiritual encounters and can win any battle in any realm. As this example shows, when Satan tried to tempt Christ three times in the desert, Jesus parried each of the temptations with quotations from Scripture that precisely matched and parried with a deadly thrust at each of the devil's jabs:

- "Man shall not live by bread alone; but man lives by every *word* that proceeds from the mouth of the LORD." (Deuteronomy 8:3 NKJV, emphasis added)
- "You shall not tempt the LORD your God." (Deuteronomy 6:16 NKJV)
- "You shall fear the LORD your God and serve him." (Deuteronomy 6:13 NKJV)

Christ the Divine Warrior is the Master Swordsman. His final thrust sent the devil scurrying, and Christ was left alone as the victor.

But we must use *God's* words. Our words alone are not imbued with power. While Jesus can rebuke the devil (such as when He told Satan in Luke 4:8, "Get thee behind me, Satan" [KJV]; and in Zechariah 3:2 when the Lord said to Satan, "The LORD rebuke thee, O Satan; even the LORD that hath chosen Jerusalem rebuke thee" [KJV]), Satan will not flee from us simply because we tell him to. Rather, we must *resist* him before he will flee (James 4:7 says, "Resist the devil, and he will flee from you"

[KJV]) and and such resistance must invoke the sword/Word of God. The devil will retreat from you only by the power of God in His words as He speaks them through you in the midst of your temptation and trials.

Here are some examples of a word from the Word:

- *I can do all things through Christ who strengthens me!* (Philippians 4:13 NKJV)
- *All things work together for the good to those who love the Lord and are called according to His purpose!* (see Romans 8:28)
- *Don't fret over those who are evil, for they will soon be cut down!* (see Psalm 37:1–2)
- *God shall supply all my needs according to His riches and glory in Christ Jesus!* (see Philippians 4:19)
- *If God is for us, who can be against us?!* (Romans 8:31 NIV)
- *The One who is in me is far greater than anyone or anything in this world!* (see 1 John 4:4)

It is in the Word of God that we learn the principle and value of passing the generational blessing in a chain that began with the Creator in Genesis 1:28 ("God blessed them" [NIV]). He provided His creation children, Adam and Eve, with the blessing of life and the resources to live that life and then pass it on to the next generation.

Dr. Tony Evans puts it this way:

The true definition of a blessing is that God provides the resources for what He asks you to do. It involves both enjoying and extending His provision in your life. The blessing is not only for the parents; it is also for the benefit of the children who would then bring about the expansion of God's image in His people. This blessing enabled Adam and Eve to fill the earth and also to extend God's blessing throughout the land to those who came after them as they established families of their own. That same blessing is there for you, too, in your parenting role.[11]

The generational chain of blessing was in the divine plan of God. The family was created by God as a conduit of blessing, providing both the opportunity and framework for individuals to collectively carry out His plan in history.[12]

Satan realizes that the attack on the family is the fundamental strategy to thwart the eternal plan of God, which is to fill the whole earth with His glory (see Psalm 72:19). The first signal to Satan that he would be defeated in this spiritual war was that the power and authority of God's rule over him would be passed from generation to generation, from parent to child.

Tony Evans states it like this: "Children are the divinely ordained means of bringing the world under the dominion of Jesus Christ."[13] The plan of God is to fill the earth with His glory. The process of filling the earth with His glory is transgenerational, from us to our children, and from our children to our grandchildren, and so forth into future generations.

With the creation of Adam and Eve, it was *game on*. When God said the final "Let there be" (referring to Adam and Eve), He might as well have said, "Let the games begin!" The announcement and creation of the first son and daughter of God launched a pattern of generational blessing in the earth realm that signaled the cosmic battle between light and darkness, between good and evil, between the Divine and the demonic. Though we are positioned in the crossfire of this cosmic battle, we are participants nonetheless. But when we draw the sword of the Spirit, the Word, the *rhema* word of God, we are equipped to fight the battle.

We're in this war for the glory of the kingdom of God and for our children. The key to your victory is for you to learn how to utilize *a* word from within *the* Word in your battle. And if you have a challenged or intermittent memory to pull out a word from the Word, then take heart: Jesus Himself says in John 14:26 that the Holy Spirit, "whom the Father will send in my name, will teach you all things and will remind you of everything I have said to you" (NIV).

You have a war to tend to, Christian. And let me tell you what this war is good for: *absolutely everything*. Because it's a war for the souls of our future generations.

## CHAPTER 9

# TAKE THEM
# TO THE MOUNTAIN

*He said to his servants, "Stay here with the donkey*
*while I and the boy go over there. We will worship*
*and then we will come back to you."*

GENESIS 22:5 NIV

As we have learned, fewer children nowadays are growing up in *churchgoing* homes. Even the term *religious traditions* seems to have a murkier meaning now than in previous generations. I'm not even referring to specific denominational distinctions in style and content or in theological symbolism. I'm talking about any regular or even periodic gathering of generations for a spiritual purpose. I'm referring to the ever-widening chasm between a worshiping generation and its progeny.

I used to live in the hectic heart of Los Angeles in a part of town that left an image in my memory that often brings me a mixture of emotions. Sometimes it's a feeling of impressed admiration. Other times it's a feeling of envious reflection. In my neighborhood on any given weekend, beginning on Friday afternoon, people could be seen walking down the street, strolling past corner grocery stores and barbershops and beauty salons, grouped at an intersection, waiting for a pedestrian walk sign to change. Modestly but well-dressed men wore black suits, white shirts, fedoras, or (for the more distinguished gentlemen with full beards) elegant top hats with round, can-shaped crowns or, even more occasionally, hats with a dark fur trim. Children were often laughing or joking or playing with one another, holding the hand of a parent or walking at a dignified pace alongside them as the families proceeded on their journeys to their places of worship.

*Families*, together.

And therein lies what captures the attention of my wistful

memories: the generational passing of a tradition of worship. My contemporary neighbors were reenacting not just family togetherness but a journey to worship. It was a modern vision of the musical scenes from sections of the Psalms known as songs of ascent or degrees, which were sung during the pilgrimage of the Jews to Jerusalem. Coming around the Kidron Valley, they would fill the corridors between the mountains with strains of worship as they headed for the Temple Mount to worship. Such was the case with Abraham when he passed the blessing of worship to his son Isaac.

The greatest increasing religious demographic in America today is not Islam, as many suggest. It is clear that for many years the so-called mainline denominations have been dwindling. Although those in the Pentecostal-Charismatic denominations have been experiencing comparative growth, even they do not claim the distinction of being the fastest-growing category of people with a religious inclination. Recall the "nones" from a previous chapter, referring to people who identify as atheists, agnostics, or no religion—they make up roughly 23 percent of the US adult population while the Christians and church-affiliated population fell to 71 percent (and only 65 percent among millennials). Why is this?

I believe this degradation of spiritual values is because we seem to have arrived at a generation that has dropped the spiritual ball of worship. Or, maybe even more tragically, the ball was never passed to them by the generation preceding them.

My children are all grown. A psychologist friend, whom I employed during a very rough patch in my relationship with my youngest daughter (who was thirty at the time), told me during one $240 per hour session with him, "You can't parent grown children the way you would when they were younger." I thought, *Duh—I should know that already!* Having considered myself a somewhat learned man, both academically (with four earned degrees) and as a student of life and observer of people (as pastor of a church of a few thousand), I felt exasperated. Not because my illumination had come at a pretty hefty fee, but because of the reality that my involvement with my children had come to a season of minimal interaction and rested almost solely upon whatever positive influence I'd had on them during their formative years. Whatever major influence I had (or had not) deposited within them before they became grown adults, I would have to live with.

That realization shocked me, frightened me, and painfully enlightened me. I believe Abraham did a better job with his kid than I'd done with mine (of course, things were different in his time). I was determined to do all I could to be a better parent from then on.

The first use of the word "worship" is found in the story of Abraham and his son Isaac in Genesis 22:5. The Lord told Abraham to take his only son to the mountain and offer him as a sacrifice. This mountain was in the region of Moriah, probably Mount Moriah, a mountain that would later become the location of Solomon's temple. For Abraham, it would be the location of a most tender scene with his son.

God told Abraham to take Isaac up and, as it is stated in the King James Version of Genesis 22:2, "Take now thy son . . . and offer him there for a burnt offering." Or, as the New International Version puts it, "Sacrifice him there as a burnt offering." Abraham had been tested nine times before this. In some ways, this tenth test would be his most difficult.

Some would claim God didn't actually tell Abraham to "kill" Isaac, but the text is clear, even in the vernacular of the times: God instructed him to sacrifice as a burnt offering his precious, only begotten "miracle" child (and to do so in the same hills of Moriah in Jerusalem where God would one day in the distant future sacrifice His only begotten Son). The test had to be real or it would be no test. It had to be couched as a command, even though God knew what the outcome would be. There could be no wiggle room in the order, no parsing of the edict. Indeed, if it were merely a request, there would be room for discussion.

Imagine the conversation initiated by God if, instead of *telling* Abraham, He had asked him, "Hey, Abe, what do you think about the idea of killing Isaac for Me? Would you mind doing that?"

"What?! *Why?* That sounds sorta . . . *crazy*, Jehovah."

"Well, I'm only saying if I *asked* you, would you?"

"I don't know, God. Hey, didn't You get mad at those people in Leviticus who sacrificed their children to Molech? I don't feel comfortable going around killing innocent children, no matter how politely I'm asked."

"This would be more of a sacrifice . . . you know, for *Me*."

"For You, or *to* You? There's a difference, You know."

"Either way is good for Me. Just asking."

"Hmm . . . that's a big ask, Lord. Maybe we could come up with a different sacrifice?"

Obviously, that conversation would never have taken place; it wasn't Abraham's style to question God by that point in his

TAKE THEM TO THE MOUNTAIN

life. But if it was just a suggestion, stern or otherwise, it would have been a quick conversation. Any good dad would have politely tabled the idea and moved on to another topic if it had been just a *what-if* discussion.

Yet, it could not be a polite request either, because this was a test of Abraham's faith, a test of his willingness to utterly comply, a test of his total belief in God and his trust in God's word. However, God already knew Abraham had developed an obedient faith in Him; which means this test was actually not for God to see if Abraham would be obedient—it was for Abraham *himself,* so he could see his own faith in action and would know to a living certainty that he would be a faithful leader, no matter what lay ahead.

Abraham's response was immediate: early the next morning, he saddled up, willing to give up his son—something far more difficult to do than sacrificing one's self.

The greatness in Abraham was displayed in the fact that he was willing to give up his son for God. Just as God would one day give up His Son for humankind.

> They arrived at the place to which God had directed him. Abraham built an altar. He laid out the wood. Then he tied up Isaac and laid him on the wood. Abraham reached out and took the knife to kill his son. (Genesis 22:9–10 MSG)

By this time in his life, Abraham had come to know God very well. He knew God would never issue a frivolous command and that He had a purpose for everything. More importantly, he knew God had made a promise to Abraham that his seed would be as countless as the sand on a seashore. With Isaac dead, that would mean God would have to break a promise—something He is incapable of doing.

Abraham made a profound announcement at the foot of that mountain. He instructed his companions to wait at the bottom of the hill while he and Isaac went to the mountain to "worship." He not only said they would go, but that they would *return*. Abraham knew God would either resurrect Isaac or create an identical, brand-new Isaac or stop his hand from slaying Isaac or provide another sacrifice in place of him. That is a learned, unquestioning faith in God. Faith to a *knowing*.

As for Isaac himself, this was an amazing young man. He was no mere child at the time but probably in his midteens. So after the porters reached the base of the mountain and Abraham took the wood for the sacrifice and placed it on Isaac (somewhat as Christ carried His own cross), father and son proceeded alone up the hill. So, upon arriving at the spot where Abraham started to bind Isaac (Genesis 22:9), why did Isaac not take off running, as any other hardy lad would do? And why, when Abraham laid him, bound, on the altar on top of the wood and took out that knife, did Isaac not roll off of the wood and struggle up and run away? If the entire exercise was only a suggestion, a polite request from God and not an instruction, then why didn't Isaac try to talk some sense into his father? Why didn't he point out to Abraham, "Hey, Dad—it wasn't a *command* from God; it was only a *suggestion*. Now get me outta here!"?

Here's why it wasn't that way: a baton (or generational blessing lesson) released must be a baton received. Abraham had taught and demonstrated worship and faith while he and Sarah raised Isaac. Because of the generational blessing of good parents who lived out and displayed in the sight of their child the attributes of utter faith in God's commands, Isaac trusted his father just as his father trusted God, which meant Isaac utterly trusted God too. Even to the point of being a willing sacrifice.

Not many are willing to give up their children at the suggestion of a benevolent and loving person, even from God Himself. But Abraham's greatness was that even if he had not been commanded by God to sacrifice his only son, if God had only asked him a hypothetical question, "Would you do it if I asked you?" he would have been willing. For the record, I'm not sure I have that kind of faith. I would really have to have a conversation with the Lord on this one. Let's see . . . *You gave me this son, and now You want me to give him up? Give him up by taking his life?* I would really struggle with that one. I'm not sure I would have that kind of faith. Maybe that's why Abraham made the hall of faith!

If Abraham had not willingly followed the instructions, he and Isaac would not have experienced the awesome lesson of their utter and complete faith and obedience to a potentially terminal request from God. *Sacrifice him.* They may have felt afraid inside as they marched to carry out the task; any normal human would. But the text doesn't give us their state of emotion, only their frame of mind. They didn't grumble, didn't complain, didn't refuse or struggle or run or beg or whimper. They did as they were told by a God they *knew* loves them unconditionally and permanently.

Whatever else happened on that mountain, it was the place

of worship between a father, his son, and their God. However, as we zoom in on this mountaintop drama and listen in, it also gives us insight into the components of true worship.

Remember, when Abraham leaves his entourage at the base of the mountain, he tells them he and Isaac are going to the top of the mountain, where they will worship. Father and son climb the mountain with supplies. They take a small pile of wood, which is placed on the back of the young, robust Isaac. They take a little lamp of fire and a knife (Genesis 22:6). Evidently Abraham had given Isaac instructions as to the requirements for worship, because when they choose a place on the mountain, Isaac takes inventory. He says, "Dad, we have the fire, we have the wood, we have a knife . . . but something's missing. *Hmm.* Fire. Wood. Knife. Fire. Wood. Knife. . . . Daddy, something is missing. We have the fire, check. We have the wood, check. We have the knife, check. But where's the lamb? Daddy, you said we were coming to worship. You taught me that in order to have true worship, we must have a lamb; we must bring an offering. We have the fire, we have the wood, we have the knife, but where is the lamb? We can't have true worship without the lamb. Where's the lamb?" (see v. 7 NIV).

*Where is the lamb?*

That question echoes down the corridors of time. It ricochets down the side of the mountain. *Where is the lamb?* It crisscrosses over generations of worship seekers. *Where is the lamb?* It bounces off the words of prophetic utterances of major and minor prophets. *Where is the lamb?* It hovers over the four-hundred-year chasm of intertestamental prophetic silence. *Where is the lamb?* It meanders down the valley of the Jordan River until one day John the Baptist—an eccentric man of God with little interest in making a fashion statement—is dipping and dunking people in the baptismal waters of the ancient river when he looks over the mound of the horizon and sees One who walked as no man walked. John hears the prophetic question, *Where is the lamb?* and, looking at the figure entering the baptismal scene, he declares: "[There He is! There He is!] Behold! The Lamb of God who takes away the sin of the world!"(John 1:29 NKJV).

YOU CANNOT HAVE TRUE WORSHIP WITHOUT THE LAMB OF GOD!

And that lamb is Jesus the Christ.

## BATON RECEIVED

In the passage below, when Isaac himself built an altar many years after the sacrifice scene with him and his father on Mount Moriah, Isaac may have had flashbacks as he recalled that day on the mountain and the example that was set by him and his father, Abraham:

> From there he went up to Beersheba. That night the LORD appeared to him and said, "I am the God of your father Abraham. Do not be afraid, for I am with you; I will bless you and will increase the number of your descendants for the sake of my servant Abraham." Isaac built an altar there and called on the name of the LORD. There he pitched his tent, and there his servants dug a well. (Genesis 26:23–25 NIV)

Beersheba was a very special place with special memories for Isaac. The name *Beersheba* means "the well of the oath"; it was where Abraham had once entered into a covenant with the Philistines. And now, years later, Isaac thought of his father when he built his own altar to the Lord.

The reenactment of Isaac's previous Moriah scene at Beersheba means that he essentially carried the generational baton from Moriah to Beersheba. Notice that Isaac attached a name to this worship place: *he called on the name of the Lord.* So, there was an ACT of worship, there was a PLACE of worship, and there was a NAME for worship.

For us today, it is a reminder of covenant relationship where God assures us of His presence, His encouragement, and His assistance. And it is the place of preparation for what lies ahead for us when we come down from the mountain of blissful worship.

There are many generational similarities between Abraham and his son. Their walks were each punctuated with worshiping that was highlighted by a word from God, who spoke to them both. God told Abraham where to look for the sacrifice. God told Isaac, "Do not be afraid, for I am with you; I will bless you and will increase the number of your descendants for the sake of my servant Abraham" (Genesis 26:24).

There are other generational continuity comparisons between Abraham and Isaac, and Moriah and Beersheba, and how and why Isaac's generation greatly prospered after Abraham. But it all began with Isaac witnessing his father's complete devotion and obedience to the Lord.

If you want a faith-building experience with your children, let them see how you operate in the face of the mountains we must climb in life, the walls we must scale, and the obstacles we must overcome as followers of our most high and mighty God. If you want the peaceful assurance that you have left them with a spiritual road map of how to get through literally *anything* life throws at them, then tell God you will live your life in agreement with His will, His Word, and His ways. Then you will pass mountain-overcoming skills and Abrahamic faith to your children, grandchildren, and generations beyond.

## CHAPTER 10

# TAKE
# THE STAGE

*It seems to me that God has put us
who bear his Message on stage in a theater . . .*

1 CORINTHIANS 4:9 MSG

The year was 1967. The place was the Alpha House (of Alpha Phi Alpha Fraternity) on the campus of the University of Illinois. Or maybe it was the AKA House (Alpha Kappa Alpha Sorority). Whichever it was, the lights were turned down, the room was tightly packed, and the floor was crammed with couples wrapped close—*real close*—together in one another's arms in octopus-like embraces.

Billowing from speakers was the number-six hit on the Billboard R&B chart, the only top-ten song by one of the more uniquely skilled, amazingly talented, and highly polished male groups out of Detroit, the Fantastic Four (no, not the four of the popular contemporary comic book and movie fame). The quartet eased into the tune "The Whole World Is a Stage." With a soulful *Hmm*, the lead singer's velvety voice oozed into the opening lines as dancers grooved to the beat . . .

*The whole world is a stage*
*And everybody's playing a part.*[1]

Probably few people know these lyrics are a paraphrase of act 2, scene 7 of William Shakespeare's *As You Like It*, and the title and hook line is over 350 years old (making the Bard the first to express this particular philosophical interpretation of life) . . .

*All the world's a stage,*
*And all the men and women merely players;*
*They have their exits and their entrances.*[2]

. . . Or maybe not; maybe the Fantastic Four and the Great Bard were not original with the concept of the world being a stage. Because Eugene Peterson's contemporary paraphrase of Paul's words in 1 Corinthians 4:9 seems to suggest that the great apostle predates the Bard with this same view of life. In this passage below, Paul gives the Corinthians a firsthand, realistic view of what life in ministry to the Lord Jesus is really like:

It seems to me that God has put us who bear his Message on stage in a theater in which no one wants to buy a ticket. We're something everyone stands around and stares at, like an accident in the street. We're the Messiah's misfits. You might be sure of yourselves, but we live in the midst of frailties and uncertainties. You might be well-thought-of by others, but we're mostly kicked around. Much of the time we don't have enough to eat, we wear patched and threadbare clothes, we get doors slammed in our faces, and we pick up odd jobs anywhere we can to eke out a living. When they call us names, we say, "God bless you." When they spread rumors about *us*, we put in a good word for *them*. We're treated like garbage, potato peelings from the culture's kitchen. And it's not getting any better. (1 Corinthians 4:9–13 MSG)

In the passage above, Paul is passing the baton of the blessings (and challenges) of ministry to the next generation of saints at Corinth. He wrote to them in the role of a spiritual father speaking to his spiritual children: "I am writing this not to shame you but to warn you as my dear children" (1 Corinthians 4:14 NIV; see also 2 Corinthians 6:13). He wants them to know the humbling honor of serving in the kingdom of God. But he is also speaking as a father trying to prepare his children for the realities of ministry.

Let's take a closer look at the words of Paul the thespian as paraphrased by Eugene Peterson in 1 Corinthians 4:9. Peterson possibly began with the words of the King James Version, which says: "For I think that God hath set forth us the apostles last, as it were appointed to death: for we are made a spectacle unto the world, and to angels, and to men." Notice that Peterson forms his world stage theory around exegesis of the word *spectacle*, translated from the word *theatron*, from which we get our word *theater*. Peterson has Paul comparing his ministry to being on a stage in a theater.

Thus, Paul is not necessarily speaking strictly or specifically to ministers in our contemporary idea of the man or woman who stands behind a sacred desk, often in robes and vestments (although some in a high church tradition still wear them). He is not speaking to seminary graduates or degree holders in some theological or ecclesiastical discipline. He is speaking to regular, ordinary believers. In fact, he makes it clear that he is not speaking to them in light of their spiritual maturity, for he acknowledges that they are still spiritual babes in Christ (see 1 Corinthians 3:1).

I have a friend who prays every time he stands in the pulpit as he prepares to preach to the congregation. His prayer goes something like this: "Lord, may I please You, for You are my ultimate audience." Every time I hear him say this, I am blessed, challenged, and inspired. Just as he does, I want to get beyond the common idea that the people in the congregation are the audience.

Yet, I used to sometimes flow in the flesh (regretfully) to try to please my audience. I was sincere, but I would study how other great pulpiteers "handled" a congregation with buzz phrases, strategic pauses, and dramatic gestures to *wow 'em* with a show (you may have seen one of these pulpiteers on TV or on a stage). In the African American tradition, some would "tune up" and sing or "whoop" the close of the message with exclamations like, "Ain't He all right?" or "Didn't He do it!" As legitimate as these "techniques" may be in the context of sincere spiritual celebration, I ashamedly admit that I have used them carnally and, regretfully, sometimes manipulatively. I would in essence take my eyes off the Lord and put my mind on impressing the listener rather than improving them.

I don't say this as a critique of these great men and women but as a confession of my own sincere, yet sometimes carnal, desire to please my audience, the saints in the pews. I, like my friend, tried to remind myself that "my ultimate audience is God," yet, I could never escape the reality that I actually am on a stage, engaging an audience. And that is why Paul's theology of ministry as revealed in his loving, fatherly letter to his spiritual children has given me a different perspective on the reality of ministry.

Yes, I do ultimately want to please my Father, but Paul

corrects my understanding of the "posture" of ministry. He said it is as if God has positioned His people on a stage before the world. There is a sense in which the audience is *our* audience—the audience of the world. And maybe the Fantastic Four and Shakespeare were right, that the world is a stage. As Paul said, it's like we preachers are on a stage in a theater, as if that's where the Lord has placed us who live and minister in His name. We are on the stage before the world but representing our Lord, who is the "producer" of what happens on the stage!

At Faithful Central Bible Church, we have a drama ministry made up of people who are, who have been, or who want to be in the entertainment business. When asked about the "star power" in our church, my classic response is that we have a bell-shaped ministry of performers. We have quite a few who are on the lower left side of the bell curve—those who have great dreams, exciting expectations, and undaunted hopes of being on the stage. Others are occasionally on a stage in front of cameras. Some are on a stage in front of a live audience. Many of them have come to Hollywood from various parts of the country with a determined commitment to make it big in the land where "dreams are made and some come true." Then we have a few at the top of the bell curve, people who are on the national stage or in national shows. We have a few who have won Grammys and Emmys, who are on the big stage and at the top of their game. We also have several who are on the downstroke, the right side of the curve, living off the laurels of their past stage life. Some are effective coaches to those on the opposite side of that curve, the up-and-comers. Others are writers and directors of those who are struggling and straining to both climb the ladder to the big stage and pay their bills along the way. But the common denominator is the spot-light, the stage.

Paul says we as believers are living our lives on the stage of the world. And he gives us the backstory of ministry: ministry is like God putting you on a stage in a theater where no one wants to buy a ticket. He goes on to say that they mock us, gawk at us, and make fun of us. He says they look at us like an accident in the street. They pass us like they're looky-loos, like people in bumper-to-bumper traffic on your side of the freeway watching an accident that happened over on the other side, with people stopping and staring and looking at us while they're slowly moving down the highway of life.

Paul used this theater metaphor both culturally and person-ally. There was a theater in the center of Corinth, and Paul's reference would trigger his audience's minds to focus on that familiar landmark. Having spent more time in Corinth than any other city, Paul would have been familiar with its large, fourteen thousand–seat amphitheater. Theaters and stadiums were com-monly used for athletic games and in connection with pagan rituals.

Additionally, it is possible that he had in mind his experi-ences in Ephesus. It seems he caused a riot in that ancient city, where the setting was in the large theater in the center of town (Acts 19:23–41). It is the same word Paul used in 1 Corinthians 4:9 for "spectacle" in the King James Version. He most certainly would have remembered his tumultuous time in Ephesus.

One of my favorite places to visit when I go to the Holy Land is this very theater in Ephesus. Much of the present city of Ephesus has been excavated and restored and looks just as it did in biblical times. One such restored masterpiece is the very theater spoken of in the Acts account and possibly alluded to by Paul in his letter to the Corinthians. It is there today, and I have many memorable recollections of standing, singing, and worshiping in that ancient venue.

By his use of *theatron* ("spectacle"), Paul seems to be alluding to an image of condemned men tortured and exposed to the wild animals in the outdoor theaters of the time. These people are also pictured as despised before the whole world (*kosmos*) and the angelic host. In other words, we preachers are a spectacle, something that people gawk at, gaze at, mock, criticize, critique, make fun of. It seems as though God has made us to be a spectacle, Paul says. Thus, Paul is also metaphorically describing the life of any believer, using theatrical terms. In fact, when you look back through Scripture, you will discover that the Bible is filled with theatrical words and alliterations.

## THAT'S ENTERTAINMENT

This world we are being sent into is divided into roughly seven different cultures or "mountains." One of these areas, these mountains, the enemy has set up his stronghold of control and influence over is the entertainment industry. In his website 7 Cultural Mountains, Os Hillman writes of these mountains:

In 1975, Bill Bright, founder of Campus Crusade, and Loren Cunningham, founder of Youth With a Mission, had lunch together in Colorado. God simultaneously gave each of these change agents a message to give to the other. During that same time-frame, Francis Schaeffer was given a similar message. That message was that if we are to impact any nation for Jesus Christ, then we would have to affect the seven spheres, or mountains of society that are the pillars of any society. These seven mountains are business, government, media, arts and entertainment, education, the family and religion. There are many subgroups under these main categories.

About a month later, the Lord showed Francis Schaeffer the same thing. In essence, God was telling these three change agents where the battlefield was. It was here where culture would be won or lost. Their assignment was to raise up change agents to scale the mountains and to help a new generation of change agents understand the larger story.[3]

Apostle Paul is just one example among many utilizing such theatrical motifs in the Word of God. For example, there is the following from the *Dictionary of Biblical Imagery*:

We can find dramatic performers in the Bible among the OT prophets who engaged in what today we would call street theater. Ezekiel performs the upcoming siege of Jerusalem with a model of the city and by acting out the citizens' future deprivations (Ezekiel 4–5; 12). Hosea's marriage to Gomer, Isaiah's three years of nakedness representing the future of Egypt (Isaiah 20), and Agabus's binding of himself to represent Paul's subjugation (Acts 21:11) are other symbolic prophetic performances. The master of such theater was Jeremiah (13:1–7; 17:19–27; 19; 27; 32:1–25; 51:59–64).[4]

Indeed, there are entire books that feature theatrical motifs. Street performers on Hollywood Boulevard and in Times Square might even be seen as theatrical descendants of the original street preacher, Jeremiah. Jeremiah set up a metaphorical pulpit on the corner and, as Paul alludes, spent his life preaching. And no one was saved. No one's life was changed. No one listened as they passed by this spiritual beggar, the mighty Jeremiah. Same thing happened with Ezekiel, who is featured in another Bible book rife with dramatic revelation, particularly with regard to end-times revelation.

Then there's the book of Job, which is loaded with so much drama that buying a ticket before being allowed to read it would not seem unreasonable. It's one of the saddest and most realistic books in the entire Bible. The book of Job is constructed out of dialogues (as dramas are) and has a dramatic prologue and epilogue. Job's friends, moreover, function as the chorus of ancient theatrical performances. The book (or "performance") of Job tells the story of a good and innocent man who suffered great tragedy and loss. The bulk of the book is about Job's false friends. I've had some of those characters in my life. Have you? The reality of fake friends is a scenario that many of us have played a role in.

Indeed, the books of Job and Mark, and parts of the book of Revelation, are filled with theatrical language and pictures, as the *Dictionary of Biblical Imagery* points out:

The book of Job is constructed out of dialogues, as dramas are, and has a dramatic prologue and epilogue. Job's friends, moreover, function as the chorus of ancient theatrical performances. The book of Mark has been found to resemble Greek tragedy following Aristotelian norms (Bilezikian). These norms include a prologue (Mark 1:1–15), complications (Mark 1:16–8:26), a recognition scene (Peter's confession, Mark 8:27–30) and a reversal of the fortunes of the leading character followed by the denouement (Mark 8:31–16:8). The book of Revelation likely shows the influence of Greek theater. It is filled with dramatized scenes and dialogue, characters and events placed in elaborately embellished settings, the costuming of characters, and ritualistic movement of characters, as though stage managed.[5]

It is through the entertainment industry that many of our values are created and shaped. This industry tells us what to buy, it guides what we celebrate, it shapes what we value and patronize. It is this theatrical context that Paul uses to describe what ministry is all about. The more you read, the more the pictures, portraits, and comparisons with the theatrical world reveal themselves in the Bible.

Again, from that rich minefield, the *Dictionary of Biblical Imagery* . . .

The Song of Songs, for example, contains an abundance of dialogue, and the characters are characteristically placed in specific settings (in fact, dramatic theories and even dramatizations have been offered throughout the history of this book's interpretation). The songs of Ascent, Psalms 120–134, were performed by Hebrew pilgrims on the way to Jerusalem to celebrate their traditional feasts. Psalm 124:1 and Psalm 129:1 have instructions for the participation of the pilgrims. Other passages suggest possible actions to accompany the recital of the songs: "I will lift up my eyes to the hills—From whence comes my help? My help comes from the LORD" (Psalm 121:1–2 NKJV).[6]

## THE BIBLE ACTS OUT DRAMA

The Bible is a book of drama, the telling of stories of love, evil, and redemption through the Star of His story, the Son of the living God. The Bible contains strong, rich, riveting, and poignant drama. Everywhere we turn in this book we find an abundance of quoted speeches, snatches of dialogue, positioning of characters in striking settings, and gestures by characters running the emotional gamut—anger, secrecy, fear, craziness, love, foolishness. From Genesis through Revelation, there's drama in the Bible.

My friend Leonard Sweet would probably suggest that the script for the drama of our lives is told not so much through our theology as through a "theography" (Sweet's term for the whole of Scripture as the story of Jesus from beginning to end). Sweet writes:

The end product of biblical Christianity is a person— not a book, not a building, not a set of principles or a system of ethics—but one person in two natures (divine/

human) with four ministries (prophet/priest/king/sage) and four biographies (the Gospels). But those four biographies don't tell the whole story. Every bit of Scripture is part of the same great story of that one person and that one story's plotline of creation, revelation, redemption, and consummation. . . . [H]umanity was created to find its identity in a relationship with God. The story of Jesus as found in the Bible shows us how to do that.[7]

Paul would say we tell that story on the stage of the theater of the world, the place where talent is on display. The people who act on this stage, mostly men and some women, are even called *actors*.

The Greek word for *actor* is transliterated in English as *hypocrite*. The people who performed onstage, the actors, were called hypocrites because they promoted falsehood. They had an ability to present something that was not true as though it were true. They were labeled as skilled and anointed master deceivers. In Greek times, just as today, a person was examined, scored, acclaimed, and appreciated based on how good of an actor they were. The measure of how good you were was all about the measure to which you made the spectators believe something false, something outlandish. That something became true due to the effectiveness of actors who had an ability to deceive so powerfully that it created the suspension of disbelief in the imagination of the viewers.

The actors on that stage wore minimal costumes as well. The storyline was told behind masks. Depending on the storyline, the actor would wear one or more different masks. They didn't have microphones, but there was a device in the mask that could change the intonation of the actors' speech. If they were telling a story that had a good ending, it would often be a comedy, so they'd wear a mask with a smile on it. The actor is smiling behind the mask, but not for long, because it's hot in that mask. The longer he smiles, the hotter he gets; all while the mask portrays a smile. Just as in life: pain on the inside, pleasure on the outside.

When the story was about a more serious topic, the mask would have a frown. A mask with a frown would indicate the drama is a tragedy. The skill of the actor would be in his ability to switch back and forth from one mask to another, to change his emotion by the mask he wore, in order to convince the audience that the actor was now portraying a different emotion.

With all that in mind, let's focus again on Paul's fascinating theory in 1 Corinthians 4. We are placed by God on a stage in a theater where no one wants to buy a ticket. When we go back to the beginning of the chapter, we discover that on this stage, in this theater of life where God has placed us, we are to play two roles: we are to be servants and we are to be stewards.

Below are three versions of 1 Corinthians 4:1. Notice how the third version ties them all together:

Let a man so account of us, as of the ministers of Christ, and stewards of the mysteries of God. (KJV)

This, then, is how you ought to regard us: as servants of Christ and as those entrusted with the mysteries God has revealed. (NIV)

Let a man so consider us, as servants of Christ and stewards of the mysteries of God. (NKJV)

## CHRIST:
## WARDROBE OF BIBLICAL DRAMA

Thus, we are to don the images, the wardrobes, of both servant and steward.

Let's go first to the wardrobe department. Our basic uniform is Jesus Christ. The phrases "put on" and "put off" were common in the culture of the times and are "picture words" that speak of clothing or apparel; to put on or take off clothing. They were also often used by Greek writers to refer to imitating or following the example of someone by copying his spirit to become like him.[8] Paul expresses this idea again in his letter to the Ephesians as he talks about putting off the old man and his former conduct of corrupt actions and deceitful lusts in exchange for the righteousness and holiness of Christ (Romans 13 and Ephesians 4).

Paul expands this idea in his letter to the Galatians by switching metaphors: instead of putting on Christ, he says we are baptized into Him. The word for *baptize* carries the idea of being immersed into something; in this case, immersed into the character of Christ. It is the idea of living a life that is identified with Christ (Galatians 3:27). When he writes to the saints at Colossae, he again changes metaphors to express the same idea. He says they are to put on love as they would put on a suit of clothing (Colossians 3:14).

In Ephesians 6:11 and 13, Paul gives us our last piece of uniform, "the whole armor of God" (NKJV); then he goes on in verses 14 through 17 to list the armor—our uniform. One note about this spiritual armor: Paul's description of this piece from the holy wardrobe department located in these verses reveals that there is no armor protecting the soldier's back. In other words, we are to never turn our backs on our stance as men and women of God.

## THE STAGE OF LIFE

Now that we are dressed, we leave the wardrobe department and make our way to the stage. It is of the utmost importance that you take your place in the light. The stage is set and your mark is center stage in the key light. Lighting comes from two places: there are lights from above and there are stage lights. The lights from above are adjustable, and the lighting director has made sure that wherever you move on the stage, you are still in the light (see Psalm 27:1, "The LORD is my light" [NIV]; and Matthew 5:14, "You are the light of the world" [NIV]). As you move across the stage, you walk from side to side in the light (see Isaiah 2:5). This is akin to the old hymn "Jesus, the Light of the World," which was sung in my parents' church choir as a processional:

> *We'll walk in the light*
> *Beautiful light.*
> *Come where the dewdrops of mercy shine bright.*
> *Shine all around us by day and by night.*
> *Jesus, the Light of the World.*

Likewise, we are to live in the heavenly Light (which is God; see 1 John 1:5 and Revelation 21:23).

But there is also stage lighting. Where you stand is lit by you—you are the light of the stage/world just as God is the Light of the world (John 8:12 and 9:5). Maybe you remember this little Sunday school song:

*This little light of mine, I'm gonna let it shine*
*This little light of mine, I'm gonna let it shine*
*This little light of mine, I'm gonna let it shine*
*Let it shine; let it shine; let it shine.*

One of the verses of the song speaks of shining this light "all in my home." In this stage performance, I would suggest adjusting the line to "all on my stage." In other words, let it shine everywhere you go.

Part of the challenge of living for the Lord on the stage of life is to be such a light that shines in the darkness. But another part of the challenge is to shine through *your own* darkness. That is, in those times when you can't see your way out or your way through, or when you're trying to shine through tears and heartache and pain. *Let it shine, let it shine, let it shine*, no matter what troubles you.

Okay, so now you're on the stage. You're dressed in your stage costume. The lighting is set. You're going to play two roles: a servant and a steward. Now let's look at your character profile. Both of the words *servant* and *steward* are synonyms for servant or slave. However, neither are the more common word for *servant*, which is *diakonoi*, meaning "a servant who serves or waits at a table," kind of like an indentured waiter. This is the word that is used in Acts 6:2, referring to people known as deacons, men who display the epitome of a servant's spirit. They love the Lord, they live in the power of the Holy Spirit, and they have a calling to help people (in the case of Acts 6:1, those people who felt neglected, overlooked, forgotten).

However, the more common term for servant, *diakonoi*, is not the term used in our 1 Corinthians 4:1 text. The term used in our text for the word *servant* is *huperatai*, which is a very unique, very dramatic picture word. The root of *huperatai* means "to row," and the prefix means "under." The term stresses subordination and responsibility to a superior.[9] Its emphasis is not so much on where they serve, but their *position of service* relative to another. In other words, the *huperatai* servants are "under-rowers" in their relation to Christ.[10]

## NOW, ROW!

There is a classic movie starring Charlton Heston titled *Ben-Hur*, in which he plays a Palestinian Jew battling the Roman Empire during the time of Christ. Ben-Hur is arrested, along with his entire family, and he is made a slave.[11]

In one scene, he and a bunch of other slaves are loaded into the belly of a slave ship and seated in two rows, one on the port side, the other on the starboard side. Their job is to row the ship through the water. They are *huperatai*—"under-rowers." There is an overseer at the front of the two rows who is sitting on a stool with big drum mallets in his fists and a large drum between his legs. He keeps the beat with the drum and carefully watches the slaves to make sure they don't lag as they haul on massive oars in painful, rhythmic stokes to thrust the ship through the churning sea waves. If a slave gets tired, he is beaten by one of the other

overseers. If he dies, he is pulled off the rowing line (and probably tossed overboard) and replaced by another slave rower, all
under the scrutinizing gaze of the overseer.

These under-rowers have no control over the direction of
the ship and no say in the pace of the vessel. The overseer who
is pounding out a rhythm on the drum with the mallets is the
guy who determines the pace of the rowing. It's seldom slow, but
sometimes slower than moderate cruising speed, and often much
slower than the "ramming speed" that would require the drum-
mer to quicken his pace—and thus the speed of rowers—until
they have to abruptly stop when they hear the order shouted,
"Oars down!"

The captain rules the top deck like a stalking lion, making
sure no one is doing less than his 110 percent share. It is the captain who determines how long the journey will be and how fast
the slaves have to shove the massive boat through the waters with
their arms alone to get to the destination. The captain dictates
whether they stop, where they will stop, and how long the stop
will be. He has command of the ship. The only thing the slaves
do is row. And row. And row. That's the scene in which we play
*servants*: we are under-rower servants of our Lord (except that He
doesn't toss us overboard when we become weary).

The apostle Paul says people ought to "account" us under-
rowers as servants. He says people should be able to observe our
lives and regard them in such a manner that they come to the
logical conclusion that we are servants of the most high God.
We get our word *logical* from the Greek *logízomai*, the word for
"account." It's a mathematical term meaning "to count" or "to
calculate."[12] It suggests "drawing a conclusion with one's mind."

What kind of conclusion do people draw from observing your life? What could they conclude about how you talk, how you treat people, your value system, your spiritual priorities? Could they deduce—strictly by observation—that you are a woman or man of God?

In the next scene, we play the role of *steward*. This slave is subservient, but has responsibilities. He's a "manager of a house." He does not own the house, but he is responsible for its upkeep. He treats it as if it were his, knowing that he is ultimately accountable to the owner. There is a similar role in the annals of American slavery.

During America's dark and lamentable slave history, there were two basic classes of slave: the field slave and the house slave. The *field slave* worked the plantation and cared for the land, the livestock, and the sowing and harvesting of the crops, which were the primary sources of income for the plantation owners. But it is the other class of slave that gives an even clearer image of the roles in our text. These slaves were the *house slaves*. They worked in "the big house." They were in charge of the upkeep of their owner's house. This was the role of steward that Paul spoke of.

If you look carefully, however, you will discover what seems to be a problem with the text in 1 Corinthians 4:1. This time, let us zoom in the lens of our hermeneutical imaginations. Verse 1 gives us our roles: servants and stewards. Verse 2 then highlights the accountability of the servants: "It is required in stewards, that a man be found faithful" (4:2 KJV). But there is a syntactical problem with the flow of the two verses. Verse 1 says we play two roles, servant and steward. However, verse 2 says it is required in *stewards* that they be found faithful. A more logical and expected flow of the text might be something like, "We are servants and stewards, and it is required of servants *and* stewards that they be found faithful." However, the text implies that the requirement of faithfulness is expected of the steward but not the servant.

What might Paul be saying here? What theological and spiritual truth is contained in this apparently unbalanced couplet?

Let's go back to American slavery and look again at a fundamental difference between the two classes of slaves. The field slaves are under the constant watch of the overseer, who sets the pace and punishes anyone who falls behind. The steward, on the other hand, is given a trustful assignment of caring for the master's house—still under scrutiny, but allowed a little more freedom in accordance with the needs of their duties.

Imagine a scene on a plantation. The master of the house goes away from the house in the morning, leaving a list of chores and household duties for which the steward/house slave is held responsible while the master is away. Maybe this involves going to the market or visiting nearby plantations, whatever slave masters did during the day. And when the master returns in the evening, he comes with the expectation that the chores, assignments, and responsibilities left with the steward/house slave will have been completed. He comes home expecting to find that the steward has been faithful.

Such is the case with those of us who live on the stage, playing the two roles of servant and steward. Like the underrowing servant or the field slave, we are constantly being watched. The eyes of the skeptical world are watching us, looking for inconsistencies between our talk and our walk. The world seeks opportunities to criticize and defame the kingdom of our Lord; and it looks at our lives, as representatives of this kingdom, for evidence of a weak, ever-changing, and shallow commitment to God. It looks for incongruity between who we are in public and who we are when no one is watching (or at least when few are watching).

Your reputation is who men say you are when they examine your life. Integrity is who you are when no one is watching, when no one is there, when you are behind closed doors, behind the curtains. Integrity is who you are when you come off that stage in that public theater, when you take off your stage attire.

Thus, we play two roles. We are not only *servants*, constantly in the spotlight, but we are also *stewards* who are trusted and have been given the responsibility to care for the master's house. The Lord left His "house" (the church) in the hands of spiritual thespians like us who are to serve as under-rowers, moving His house through the ravaging opposition of the world with the assurance that the gates of hell shall not prevail against it or be able to stop it.

## THE BATON OF THE
## FAITHFUL SERVANT-STEWARD

We take the stage of life in order to pass the baton of the blessings of being servants of the living God. We take the stage to demonstrate to the next generation that there is an expected end for the faithful. We are not to be discouraged by the apathy and opposition of the world. Our lives outside of the spotlight, our lives of faithful service in the shadows, our service when no one calls our names, our lives when we have sacrificed for His name's sake, our lives of giving up the wrong for the right . . . are all being noted, regarded, and accounted by God.

Likewise with you, don't let the trials of time in the meantime discourage you. God records every offering unto Him (see Philippians 4:12–13), because one day the Master will return. And when He does, He will return with the expectation that you and I have been faithful steward-servants. And the things done in the shadows shall be brought to light and put on display before a loving God.

There is a revelation in the exhortation and encouragement of Paul in this teaching, a hidden spiritual gem of hope: you may have thought eternity will be spent praising God and rejoicing around His throne, but the jewel in the text is that when He returns, *God will praise you!* "Therefore," as it says in 1 Corinthians 4:5, "judge nothing before the appointed time; wait until the Lord comes. He will bring to light what is hidden in darkness and will expose the motives of the heart. At that time each will receive their praise from God" (NIV).

Pass the baton of service and teach the next generation that they may hear no rousing rounds of applause. They may receive few accolades or encomiums of praise in the earth realm. But those who stand tall on the stage in the theater where no one wants to buy a ticket will one day hear the greatest review of all: "Well done, good and faithful servant! You have been faithful with a few things; I will put you in charge of many things" (Matthew 25:21 and 23 NIV).

A story is told, with different variations, about a missionary who had given his life serving on the mission field. He had faithfully spread the gospel. He had taught the Word, fed the hungry, and clothed the naked. After a life of service behind the scenes of society, he and his wife took the long ship ride from Europe back to America.

On the sometimes boring days and nights in the jostling, wind-tossed boat, the missionary's mind reflected on those lonely days, the sorrowful nights, the times of opposition and persecution. Yet, he realized he would do it all over again out of his love for his Lord.

When the ship docked at the port on the shores of America, the dock was lined with waving relatives and friends of the other hundreds of passengers. As the couple slowly made their way down the gangplank, the missionary realized that there was no one there to greet him. No one waving hands, no arms of welcome. No one inquiring about his journey. No one rejoicing over the spiritual victories for which he had given his life.

Tears welled in his eyes and slowly ran down the crevices of his craggy, time-worn face as he said to his wife, "No one is here. After all those years, no one has come to welcome us home."

His wife lovingly looked up to him and with a wistful smile and a grateful heart said, "Honey, we're not home yet!"

The accolades and the "Well done, my good and faithful servant" and the trumpets of the angels will come at the end of the run, when you are lifted Home.

In the meantime, take the stage in this dark and dying world and let your light shine. Then pass the baton of the blessings of service from the Master to the next generation. Your accolades and rewards might not come when you expect them on the stage of life. But remain in character, Christian, because they will come when you arrive Home.

## CHAPTER 11

# KNOW YOUR LIMITATIONS

*I am speaking in human terms,*
*because of your natural limitations.*

ROMANS 6:19 ESV

One day I received an invitation to audition for a national television talk show. There was audition after audition, and interview after interview. When I didn't hear back for a while, I thought they had decided in favor of someone else. Then I received one more call to audition for one final round. The context of my audition situation involved me going into the mountain of media and entertainment. I'd made it to the last round; then I got a callback after that round and we went into the final round of filming.

While praying the night before, I said, "Lord, I want this if it is a platform for Your kingdom and glory—*if* it doesn't detract from my call to pastor the Faithful Central Bible Church and if money doesn't change our lifestyle."

Here's the principle: we must always go into the world with preset nonnegotiables. These nonnegotiables should be grounded in our relationship and commitment to God. Never wait until you read the script or see who is in the cast or how much you'll be paid before you determine your nonnegotiables. In other words, know where you draw the line and know your limits. Because, in the words of Inspector Harry Callahan, the iconic character made famous by actor Clint Eastwood in the movie *Magnum Force*: "A man's got to know his limitations."[1]

When I speak in the context of "natural limitations" from Romans 6:19, I am referring to our inabilities in terms of influencing or passing a blessing to the next generation. It's a reality we each must face. And there's a flip side: we must also beware not to interpret our limitations as negativities in our life. Rather, they are realities to be addressed.

The unique audition exercise I went through is related to the crucial question of how we, as Christians, go into a nation. How do Christians *"go into all the world,"* as Jesus charged us to do in Mark 16:15 (NIV)? It doesn't matter where you work or what you do; there are principles related to your going out into your various spheres of influence to do your work, to affect others, to grow and learn, to add to your experience and wisdom— all those collective blessings you would want to pass to the next generation.

I refer to these natural laws that we cannot conquer as limitations only as far as they relate to the interaction between two independent lives that are on the opposite side of the generational line. In other words, using our principle that a baton released must be a baton received, sequentially we can control the release on our side, but we can't control the reception of the other side (the next generation) in bringing continuity between the blesser and the blessee.

Put it this way: you can love a person, but you can't enforce or even control their love for you (a play on the old saying, which is probably too old for some of you to know: you can lead a horse to water but you can't make it drink). Your sincere, released love can be met with apathetic (or even practical) rejection by the object of your affections. This means that knowing our limitations with regard to the next generation is to know or to anticipate elements of the equation of the passing of the baton that we cannot control, change, or replace. That's not a negative confession; it is meant merely to challenge you to realize that there are variables that cross generation lines that we can't alter.

This is not about doubting oneself. It's not about shying away from hurdles, walls, or obstacles that are a necessary part of success. It is about recognizing that we live within the frailty and limitations of our humanity. We are all born with them. Nobody prayed for or requested them. For the most part, they are contained within the earthly realm as "natural laws" that will not yield to your Spirit-filled anointing (for example, if you step off a cliff, there is probably more than a 99 percent chance you will fall).

In desiring to pass a generational blessing forward, we must also face the limitations of our dreams for the one marked to receive our blessing. Because expecting a person to accept more than they want for themselves is setting yourself up for disappointment. For example, I once heard a senior pastor describe ministry as trying to save people who don't want to be saved, and trying to help people who don't want to be helped. Such can be the case when we are faced with the challenge of passing a blessing from one generation to a generation that has no interest in incorporating that blessing into their lives.

Such was the case with David and his son Solomon. As the king approached the end of his life, he called Solomon to his bedside to pass the baton of the blessings of God that had covered his life. Certainly, David lived a life far from perfect, but he was a man after God's heart (Acts 13:22). He had known the presence and favor of the Lord as he had walked through the valley and shadow of death (Psalm 23). He had learned that his Lord has the power to cleanse a sinful heart (Psalm 51). And far be it from him to die without passing the blessings of his walk with the Lord to his son Solomon.

As we listen in to the conversation between this prophet king and his son in chapter 2 of 1 Kings, it is interesting to note the words used in their meeting. In 1 Kings 2:1, the New King James Version, David "charged" Solomon. This is a much stronger word than giving him "instructions" as interpreted in the Good News Translation. It's even stronger than Paul's word "beseech," used in Romans 12:1 of the New King James Version. *Beseech* means to "urge, encourage, plead," even beg. But when David called Solomon into his presence to speak blessing over his life, he "charged" him. *Charge* is a verb that means to "give an order, to direct, to command."[2] No ambiguity there, no polite request. More of a direct order.

David commands his son to follow the Lord. He tells him to be strong and to walk in the ways of the same God who had covered David's life. To live under the Word of God and pay attention to the judgments and testimonies therein. However, when you track the life of Solomon, you discover that he either rejected the baton or dropped it altogether, thus robbing at least his generation of the value of David's rich and immeasurably important life lessons as Israel's true first king and a man after God's heart.

The sad part is that David died with the expectation that Solomon would heed his words. Once the transition had been made and Solomon was affirmed and positioned as king of the kingdom (1 Kings 1:43), he did appear for a while to be following in his father's footsteps. But then, as we read in 1 Kings 3:3, fissures began to emerge in his faithfulness: "Solomon loved the Lord and followed all the decrees of his father, David, except that Solomon also offered sacrifices in the high places—places of idol god worship" (1 Kings 3:3; my paraphrase).

Normally I would read the passage above as a kind of footnote that merely describes the common practice of the day—as signifying a place where pagans offered their sacrifices to their different gods, and the people of God offered theirs to Him. But the yellow warning flag is in the next verse, verse 4, which indicates that Gibeon was the most important place of worship and implies that these "high places" were exceptions to the rule during the transition period between Tabernacle worship and the full dedication of the Temple. What raises the warning flag is the negative implication in the second part of verse 3 in the word "except" (NIV). The pagan Canaanites considered the hilltops conducive to worship because they felt closer to their gods in the elevated locations and therefore felt their prayers had a shorter distance to go to reach their gods and were more likely to be heard and answered in the affirmative than the prayers of the Israelites. God's people seemed to have adopted these local worship sites as their own temporary altar sites, even though the Law given to Moses prohibited such practices (Leviticus 17:3–4).

Solomon appears to have developed a pattern of compromise by following seemingly small or generally accepted practices that had been disallowed in the Law but nevertheless had been gradually eased back into practice. Practices that would lead to his downfall.

We can see the before and after of the slipping of Solomon's values, from when he first prayed for wisdom in 1 Kings 3:9 and 5:12, and then fast-forwarding to his final days, when we learn that he had drifted away from his Lord and the legacy of his dad, David: "In this way, Solomon did what was evil in the Lord's sight; he refused to follow the Lord completely, as his father, David, had done. . . . The Lord was very angry with Solomon, for his heart had turned away from the Lord, the God of Israel" (11:6, 9 NLT).

The issue is that Solomon turned to idol gods because he was influenced by the pagan women he chose. Sequentially, we see that he began to frequent their places of worship before he took them as wives. Yet, "the Lord had clearly instructed the people of Israel, 'You must not marry them, because they will turn your hearts to their gods.' Yet Solomon insisted on loving them anyway" (11:2 NLT).

In our most sincere and dedicated efforts to pass blessings to our next generation, we must acknowledge our limitations if we want to facilitate the completion of the passing process. We can't control the hearts of the next generation. Solomon's heart turned from the Lord. He grew up in a godly home but with an imperfect godly father who had a heart for the Lord and who made every effort to walk in the ways of the Lord (even when he fell and later came to realize it, he repented). Solomon, on the other hand, went the opposite direction: he started out eager to follow the Lord, then went downhill as he got older.

## LIMITATIONS AND CONSEQUENCES

I can't even begin to count how many faithful and godly mothers and fathers have sat in the pews in a worship service with broken and bruised hearts over sons or daughters who turned from the Lord. It is even more perplexing when you see siblings raised in the same home, taken to the same church, sitting in the same Sunday school class, and one walks with the Lord while the other walks away from Him.

Many parents know what it's like to warn their children time and time again, only to see them through tearful eyes do exactly what they were warned against. I know parents whose kids are in jail, or living with a drug habit, or bearing the scars of bullet holes in their bodies. I have friends who have known the pain of advising their kids against ungodly relationships, only to see them in divorce court or family court or fighting for custody of their kids or grandkids. I know parents who have no idea where their sons or daughters are. Some have disappeared into the shadows of crime or the drug culture. Some are homeless and living in loneliness and despair, with habits that prohibit them from residing in the comfort of their parents' homes. They made their choices but could not choose the consequences. We are all subject to the limitations of transgenerational blessings.

One of my mentors, a preacher who has since passed away, once told me in a quavering voice and with melancholy eyes, "Your children can be your greatest source of joy. Your children can be your greatest source of pain." He said this while engaging a reputable lawyer to defend his son against a charge of murder. Another of his sons (also a friend of mine) was in the middle of a separation from his wife when he went to her apartment one day and, during an altercation at the door, discovered that another man was there with her. She closed the door, and my friend drove back to his own apartment and got a gun. Then he went back to the home of his wife. When she opened the door, he shot her point-blank in the head.

That is a stark and tragic story, but it highlights how we can do our best to pass the baton of righteousness and godly living to the next generation, but we cannot control the hearts of those for whom we are trying to set examples.

In the words of author Henri Nouwen in his book *The Wounded Healer*, many people are "wounded healers."[3] I know many preachers who have lived with broken hearts over children who have turned away from the Lord. All too often, we are trying to help save someone else's children while we are losing our own. I have friends whose children have been to jail, committed horrendous crimes, chosen lifestyles of ungodliness. Many times there has been a scenario of negligence on the part of the holy parent. Many pastors' kids and ministers' kids feel tremendous pressure simply because their father is the Right Reverend So-and-So, or their mother is Prophetess Pastor So-and-So.

Ephesians 1 says we have been called by God and are predestined to walk within the call on our lives. In verse 4, Paul says we were chosen by God before the foundation of the world, which means God chose us to have a relationship with Him before Genesis 1:1, before He established the foundation way back in eternity past. Still, you can do all you can to set a godly example for your children, but you can't always influence them to follow that example. Your limitation with them is that you cannot control their hearts and you can't control their path. This is because we may have been called, but we still have the intellectual ability to reject that call, because salvation does not nullify volition.

I am continually amazed by the power of the love of a God who loves us enough to give us the choice and the ability not to love Him. We are accepted in the beloved, but He gives us the ability to reject Him, the will *not* to choose Him. That's how much He wanted the possibility of true, authentic *relationship* with us as individuals who could choose whether to love Him, accept Him, believe in Him, follow Him, or not. Now *that* is true love. And only true love offers the possibility of true, personal relationship.

God predestined us to a relationship with Him, according to His will. The word *predestined* is a compound word with a root that means "to determine or decree." The prefix means "before or prior to." The prefix and the root give the idea of marking out a boundary or setting a limit beforehand. So the Lord predetermined that a life lived according to His will is one that is lived within preset boundaries or limits. However, Paul acknowledges that man has the intellectual cognitive ability and the free will choice to overrule or reject a life within those boundaries.

In the case of Solomon, David tried to pass the baton of the blessings of God to his son—who did follow within those preset boundaries for a while, but then chose to compromise his way off the path laid out by God. Such is the dilemma we, too, face when we sincerely try to pass blessings across generation lines. We can release, but they can reject and can choose not to receive. Therefore, we must recognize that we have limitations when it comes to influencing and encouraging the reception of God's will, God's way, and God's Word into the lives of others— including our own kids, raised in our own homes.

We are also limited in our ability to *influence* their choices. It is often difficult for parents to realize that there is an expiration date on their influence. Psychologist Dr. Carl Pickhardt brings this home in his study of adolescent children:

> The child (up to ages 8–9) admires, even worships parents for the capability of what they can do and the power of approval that they possess. The child wants to relate on parental terms, enjoy parental companionship, and imitates the parents wherever possible. The child wants to be like and to be liked by these adults who are mostly positively evaluated (assuming they are not damaging or dangerous to live with). A child identifies with parents because they provide the primary models to follow after and to live up to.[4]

A parent has about nine years (through the single digits) to sow seeds of righteousness, establish a godly atmosphere in the home, and instill a groundwork of biblical values in the next generation. The parent is the focus and source of information, the example of life values, and the resource for navigating the challenges of the world. However, as a child nears those double digits, things begin to change, as Dr. Pickhardt explains:

> Now comes adolescence (beginning around ages 9–13) and parents get kicked off the pedestal. In the girl or boy's childhood they could do no wrong, come adolescence it seems they can do no right. What has caused

this sudden fall from grace? Have parents changed? No, but the child has, and with cause.[5]

To be fair, we must point out that the degree of influence on a child's development is tilted when fathers are present and involved, as this quote from an article titled "A Parent's Influence" states:

> Swiss researchers discovered that if Dad faithfully attends church, even though Mom doesn't, kids are still 44 percent more likely to keep going to church as adults. But if Mom goes regularly and Dad never shows up, only 2 percent of the kids continue to attend. That's a very big gap, and a telling sign of why the father's influence is so significant.[6]

I don't mean to sound like a prophet of doom and gloom. There is still hope, and we should never discount the power of God to influence and guide our children. But when it comes to kids, parents should do more than keep them in church. Meeting their children's spiritual needs goes beyond attending worship services and must be a priority for every parent. Dr. Janice Crouse of the Beverly LaHaye Institute explains:

> The relationship that parents establish with their children determines—to a very large extent—their outcomes. If we, as parents, don't feed their souls, they will seek to fill that emptiness with drugs, alcohol, or sex—or they will

turn to the dozens of other ways teens mess up their lives by seeking a parental and faith substitute.[7]

Just as the love of God does not negate our free will, regret over the choices we make does not negate the consequences of those choices. Parents learn that their children will make choices that come as package deals with built-in consequences. While we can make our own choices, we can neither influence the consequences of our choices nor interfere in the God-given free will of the next generation in their response to our choices. Each generation begins with a clean slate that the previous generation can only pray the current generation fills with the blessings of the previous.

Take the ultimate example of them all, in Genesis 2:17, when God told Adam that if he ate the fruit of the tree of the knowledge of good and evil, he would surely die. Adam and Eve were basking in the favor, love, and covering of their Creator, who created them to fill the world with His glory. Then they chose to step outside the boundaries God had established. When we choose to deliberately disobey God, something will die. Obviously, Adam and Eve did not die immediately in the natural sense (and the theological implications of their spiritual death is an entirely different book), but the point God makes is that there are consequences that are inextricably woven within the fabric of our choices. Consequences that all too often cannot be undone and must be seen through.

There is an interesting passage that spotlights this truth in the book of Jeremiah, when the prophet tells the people they have refused to hear the word of the Lord, because they turned their hearts from God and chose to reject His word in favor of worshiping idols. Their rebellious choice brought catastrophe upon them and put them under the judgment of God. Because they chose to reject Him and His word, He sentenced them to seventy years of captivity. It's as if the Lord said, "You chose to worship idols, so here's the consequence of your choice: Israel and her neighboring lands will serve the king of Babylon for seventy years." They made the choice, but they could not choose to negate the consequences. They had to ride out their exile under the rule of the Babylonians for seventy years. This was their consequence, the sentence imposed upon them, for breaking the Law of God.

At the time, there was a prophet from Gibeon in town whose name was Hananiah. In Jeremiah 28:2–3, Hananiah said, "This is what the LORD of Heaven's Armies, the God of Israel, says: 'I will remove the yoke of the king of Babylon from your necks. Within two years I will bring back all the Temple treasures that King Nebuchadnezzar carried off to Babylon'" (NLT). *Wait a minute.* I thought the Lord Himself just said, "Israel and her neighboring lands will serve the king of Babylon for seventy years." If the Lord had said seventy years, why did Hananiah reduce their sentence by sixty-eight years?

Let's unpack this prophetic dilemma and try to figure out who got it wrong.

First, before we come down too hard on brother Hananiah, let me try to put another view to this guy. Most scholars suggest that Hananiah was a false prophet. He most certainly was wrong on the length of the sentence God had imposed, but I wouldn't be too quick to pile onto the false prophet labelers.

There was another prophet, a fellow by the name of Elijah, who did battle with 450 prophets. These 450 prophets are identified as "prophets of Baal" (1 Kings 18:19 NIV). They met Elijah on Mount Carmel and there was a dramatic battle of the prophets. The prophets of Baal called on their god. After mocking the silence of their idol god, Elijah stepped up and called out, "LORD, the God of Abraham, Isaac and Israel . . ." (v. 36 NIV). Now remember, the opposing prophets had called upon the name of their false god, Baal. I suggest therein lies a significant distinction: the prophets of Baal prophesied in the name of a *false god* (which means that they were in fact false prophets), whereas Elijah prophesied in the name of the true God of the universe, the Almighty Jehovah God.

Therefore, if Hananiah was a true prophet of Jehovah, then it might be more accurate to call him a hit-and-miss prophet. Yet, even that can come with dangers, limitations, and consequences.

Certainly Hananiah was wrong. God said seventy years, so it's seventy years. Period. End of story. In fact, I love the response of Jeremiah to Hananiah's prophecy of a reduced two-year sentence. Jeremiah said, "Amen! May your prophecies come true! I hope the LORD does everything you say" (Jeremiah 28:6 NLT). Translation: *We'll see about that.* When it indeed turned out to be seventy years, it was clear Hananiah was wrong. It turned out he hadn't actually heard from God in this case. However, again I submit that he was not necessarily a "false" prophet (that is, a prophet who knowingly prophesies falsely by the name of God). He was a prophet of the Lord. But in this case, his prophecy, his so-called word from the Lord, turned out wrong—even though he was a prophet who prophesied in the name of the true

God (although there are no other instances in the Bible where Hananiah prophesied anything, accurately or otherwise).

One of the men who influenced my life was a white-maned Arkansas man of God named Dr. B. J. Willhite. Once, when commenting on a preacher who was spiritually and theologically off base, Dr. Willhite said, "That man just missed God." I was about to affirm his observation when he continued, "But don't worry; sooner or later we all miss God" (not that we all claim to be prophets, however).

Hananiah missed God. He sincerely wanted to encourage the people. He believed he had a word from the Lord. But he was wrong. How many sincere preachers, prophets, evangelists have spoken a so-called "word from God" about someone's destiny, about someone's healing, about the will of God for someone's life? Certainly there are charlatans, there are Elmer Gantrys, and definitely there are the shysters and the crooks. But there are also sincere men and women who are sincerely wrong. They may speak a word of encouragement. They may speak a word to inspire faith. But they are wrong. They may say, "Thus saith the Lord" when the Lord hath saith no such thing. Prophets who missed God. I believe that what is so discouraging is that most of these Hananiahs don't have a Jeremiah to call them out. They are sincere, but sincerely wrong. Not false prophets, but prophets who prophesy falsely. To paraphrase Dr. Willhite, Hananiah missed God.

I believe Hananiah wanted to encourage the people that they would not have to suffer long—at least, not as long as God had said. Notwithstanding that, there are consequences for missing a prophecy supposedly quoted as being a word God had said.

Indeed, there was a severe consequence suffered by Hananiah for his prophetic limitation. Jeremiah told him: "Hear now, Hananiah; The LORD hath not sent thee; but thou makest this people to trust in a lie. Therefore thus saith the LORD; Behold, I will cast thee from off the face of the earth: this year thou shalt die, because thou hast taught rebellion against the LORD. So Hananiah the prophet died the same year in the seventh month" (Jeremiah 28:15–17 KJV).

Hananiah paid the ultimate price for missing that one prophecy. And in Deuteronomy 18:20, God Himself explains why this happened: "But the prophet, which shall presume to speak a word in my name, which I have not commanded him to speak, or that shall speak in the name of other gods, even that prophet shall die" (KJV).

And here again is our principle: in our sincere desire to pass blessings from one generation to the next, we must face the limitation of consequences. We cannot control the consequences of choices that reject the baton or the blessing that is passed. Beware of trying to deliver someone who is under the judgment of God. Beware of trying to bail out someone who has been sentenced by God. God is still at work in their lives, and the lessons He wants to teach them and the correction he wants to make on their paths cannot be negated before they have worked God's purpose.

There is an old gospel song in the African American tradition that says, "You can't hurry God. Oh no. You just have to wait." This is not merely an exhortation for those who are waiting for a blessing or some positive response of God; it is also a word for those who have chosen a way that leads away from Him. In these instances, they are on a path that is ordered by God, and

He won't bring them out of it until they have learned the lessons God wants to teach them.

Sometimes God doesn't merely bring you out of something; He brings you through it. He will bring you through the judgment period in His own time; and He will leave you there until you "come to yourself," turn (*repent*), and return to Him. You can't rebuke the judgment. You can't bypass the consequences of your choice. He can still bless you and provide for you while you are under the judgment. He can still show you mercy and grace, and you may still retain the talent He gave you, but He will not adjust judgment to your timetable. It goes back to what we've been studying: you can choose your choices, but you can't choose the consequences of your choices.

As I mentioned, I grew up in East St. Louis, Illinois (not St. Louis, Missouri—there's a big difference). Our home was always filled with extended family. We had a three-bedroom, one-bathroom house. I remember one season when my brother and sister and I slept in the same room, and in the bedroom next to ours were my cousin, her husband, and her two girls. Looking back, I have no idea how that worked, yet it was a home filled with joy and fun. On Sundays, the rule in our house was *everybody* had to go to church.

As I look back, I'm sure some of our temporary tenants probably were inspired to look for jobs faster or work more than one job to exit our house. Because my parents were always taking in or helping somebody, and it could get pretty crowded. (That's probably where my sister and I got our spirit of giving.)

On alternate years, we would visit our cousins in Detroit, or they would visit us. One year a cousin of mine who was close to my age and was also a close friend was having a rough time in her hometown, getting hooked up with the wrong crowd, hanging out with people of bad influence. She was drifting into a wayward life, so she asked if she could come live with us. My mother truly believed she could help her niece, whose mom felt she would do better in the environment of a "good Christian home" with us. So off to East St. Louis she went.

After a few weeks, the *everyone must go to church on Sundays* routine was not working for my cousin. She found her way into the East St. Louis drug scene. Soon, she began stealing from my mom. My mother helped her get a low-income apartment, but she was evicted from there. We began to hear rumors that she was into prostitution and selling some of the drugs she was using. She was in and out of jail. It was a dark and dangerous life.

My mother wanted so much to help her and would often weep over her niece. But eventually my mom had to back off from her. Last I heard, after having lived a hard life on the streets, my cousin was in a senior citizens home for drug addicts. My mother learned that there are limitations in passing blessings to others.

In spite of that dispiriting story of a child gone wrong, there are stories that have more upbeat endings.

## THE PRODIGAL

Have you ever tried to fill in the blanks in the story of Jesus's lesson of the Prodigal Son in Luke 15? In His usual parabolic style, Jesus does not give us too many background details, but there are a few revelations that address our discussion. In Luke 15:11–12, the younger son of a man with two boys approaches his father and tells him he wants his share of the estate now, rather than having to wait for it. His father agrees, divides his wealth between his sons, and the younger son goes off to do his own thing.

The culture of the times suggests that this was probably a Jewish father who had already intended to pass on the accumulated blessings of his life to his two sons. There is no indication that the father hesitated, discussed it with the kid, or even argued to persuade his son to stay. It appears the father accepted that the son had made up his mind to take what was his and leave. The father had it in his heart to bless his son, but the son was impatient and he chose to take the blessing and go.

The story goes on to reveal the consequences of the son's choice to leave his father's house: the boy lives a life of debauchery and wild times, and ends up at rock bottom. He has gone from living high on the hog to being in the hogpin (Luke 15:13–20). The son made his choice, but he could not choose the consequences of his choices.

Once the son left, the father was limited. It appears the only thing he could do was wait. In the words of my mother, he had to "leave him in the hand of the Lord!" I like to think he waited prayerfully, possibly even clinging to scriptures such as Proverbs 22:6, "Train up a child in the way he should go, and when he is old he will not depart from it" (NKJV). I can imagine the father looking down that road each day, both expecting and wondering when the son would return home, trusting by faith that the time he had spent with his son, teaching and influencing him, would not have been in vain.

The resolution of the story does end on an upbeat note. The story says that when the son finally "came to his senses" (Luke

15:17 NIV), he decided to return to his father's house. As he was treading down the road to home, "while he was still a long way off, his father saw him and was filled with compassion for him; he ran to his son, threw his arms around him and kissed him" (v. 20 NIV). I could spend the rest of this book breaking down the theological implications and insights in this brief anecdote that is an obvious parabolic portrait of our loving God. But it is clearly another lesson in the principle of the limitations of passing blessings.

The response of the father as he watched and waited, and then saw his son returning and ran out to greet him, was a very uncharacteristic action by a Jewish father in that culture. He never rebuked the son. He never chastised him. Never said, "I told you so." Never said, "You shouldn't have gone away in the first place." Didn't even chasten him for blowing through his inheritance. Instead, he threw his young son a party—*with song and dance!*

I love the way James 1:5 puts it: "If you need wisdom, ask our generous God, and he will give it to you. He will not rebuke you for asking" (NLT). I also love the King James Version: "If any of you lack wisdom, let him ask of God, that giveth to all men liberally, and upbraideth not." *Upbraideth* means "to reproach, or defame, to rail against, to assail with abusive words."[8] The NLT puts it succinctly: "He will not rebuke you." In fact, return to Him and He might even throw you a party. Or let your child do what they insist on doing, then stay watchful and prayerful and they might return and let you throw them a party.

God loves and still blesses us when we mess up, when we make bad choices, when we turn from Him and His Word, when we venture off the path He sets before us. We can't adjust the time period of judgment, can't put a clock on the consequences of our choices. We are limited by the frailty of our humanity and cannot control the consequences we incur by disobedience. Likewise, when you pass blessings into the life of someone, you are limited in your ability to influence their choice of whether or not to receive them, and you are limited in your ability to impact the consequences of their choices after they make them.

But we must take into consideration how limitless is the breadth, width, length, and height of our eternal, forgiving God. The Bible says in Jeremiah 31:3 that God loves you with an everlasting love. If your bad choices, your unwitting diversions from the path of righteousness, can cause His love for you to cease, then His love isn't *everlasting*. If you can do something to stop God from loving you, then His love has limits. But His love *is* everlasting, it *does* lasts forever, and it has *no limits*.

I want to close this chapter with a word for you. If you are struggling with guilt over the path your child has taken, if you are grieved over a child who is missing, if you are blaming yourself for the way you did or did not raise your child, then know that there is no condemnation for those who belong to Christ Jesus.

If you are a mother who sees your daughter following in your footsteps and experiencing some of the same tragedies you experienced, then cling to the promise of God that there is *no* condemnation for those who belong to Christ Jesus.

If you are a father who was not there for the first step, the first day of school, the big game, the graduation, or if you're a parent who wrestles with *I coulda, I shoulda, I wish I woulda* done or not done this or that, then know this: there is *no condemnation* for those who belong to Christ Jesus.

As we have learned in this chapter, our everlasting God loves us with an everlasting love (Psalm 90:2; Jeremiah 31:3). He is the Alpha and the Omega, the beginning and the end, and the everything in between. We may live our lives with limitations, but the God we serve knows *no* limits. He will never leave you nor forsake you.

Remember the interaction between Jesus and the woman caught in the very act of adultery in John 8:11: "I do not condemn you" (GNT).

Hear the word of the Lord: "If our heart condemns us, God is greater than our heart, and knows all things" (1 John 3:20 NKJV). If you have made some bad choices and followed the wrong road, God is there, just like the father of the prodigal son, waiting to receive you. God's love for you does not cease when you take a wrong turn, follow a bad road, or get lost on your journey. His love is with you on the crooked path. His love is with you when you drop the ball. His love is with you when you fall by the wayside. His love is with you permanently. He is the God of all comfort. He is the God who heals broken hearts. He will always love you back into the glow of His glory.

We, as humans, have limitations. Yet, isn't it nice to know we have a God who has no limitations? So, fear not. We're in the best of hands.

## CHAPTER 12

# TELL
# GOD'S STORY

*In the future, when your son asks you, "What is the meaning*
*of the stipulations, decrees and laws the LORD our God*
*has commanded you?" tell him: "We were slaves*
*of Pharaoh in Egypt, but the LORD brought us out*
*of Egypt with a mighty hand."*

DEUTERONOMY 6:20–21 NIV

We wind down our study on passing a generation blessing the way we began, with a reminder of the ultimate way to pass a generation blessing: *tell God's story.*

One of the most acclaimed movies of all time is *The Ten Commandments.* The story of Moses in that film is the story of God and His blessings on a people from one generation to the next. Moses summarizes the story of God moving from generation to generation by saying God did it all with His mighty hand, because He is God. In this context, reading Deuteronomy 6:20–21, Moses is looking back at his journey as he stands before the people of God, exhorting them to pass the truth and reality of the great blessings they have received from God to their sons and grandsons.

God blesses transgenerationally from one generation to the next. In our walk with God, the passing of the blessings is not a suggestion; it's not an additional optional extra. It's a *command,* a mandate to those who have been blessed. And the blessing is not only to be passed to your children, but also to your children's children.

## THE MIGHTY HAND OF GOD

A dear friend of mine is a Jewish rabbi. He says that in the Jewish culture, Deuteronomy 6 is the most important chapter in all of Scripture. It is the foundation upon which rests the very culture of the people of God. This passage, which lays out the purpose of the Law and comes with an exhortation to obey it, speaks about the passing of blessings. It is where Moses reviews and tells the story of what God has done.

Deuteronomy 6:20–21 rehearses and repeats the experiences of a father, who is to share them with his son, and from his son to his grandson. This passage is permeated with an atmosphere of honor, respect, and awe of God, and gives us several insights into a relationship and the blessing of that relationship being passed from one generation to another. In it, Moses is summarizing and synthesizing the Israelites' journey through a word picture of the hand of God. He says, *God brought us out, and He did it with His mighty hand.*

My rabbi friend said Deuteronomy is to be taught, read, and shared with the next generation as a recollection of the experiences it recalls as blessings that flowed from the lessons, which are to be passed forward. This is why we are not to read this chapter of the Bible as mere historical observation or recitation, but as experiential participation. The action experienced was the action of the very hand of God. Thus, our lives are to be a demonstration of His mighty hand. *We were slaves of Pharaoh in Egypt, but the Lord brought us out of Egypt with a mighty hand.*

As I explain in my book *In His Image*,[1] some aspects of God's behavior are specific to particular anatomical parts. For example, in Scripture the hand, arm, and fingers are sometimes mentioned together, and often the concepts expressed by them are interchangeable. With regard to creation, in Jeremiah 32:17, the prophet said, "Ah, Sovereign LORD, you have made the heavens and the earth by your great power and outstretched arm" (NIV). Jeremiah ascribed the workings of God's miraculous power to His arm.

Although the hand, arm, and finger are all common biblical images of power, the finger carries with it the added connotation of *authority*. In Psalm 8:3, King David looked at the same act of God as the work of God's fingers. When God sent a plague of lice upon Egypt, Pharaoh's magicians called it an act perpetrated by "the finger of God" (Exodus 8:19 NIV). It was the finger of God that inscribed the Ten Commandments on tablets of stone in Exodus 31:18. And, in Luke 11:20, it was by "the finger of God," that Jesus cast out demons while proclaiming, "No doubt the kingdom of God is come upon you" (KJV).

The hand of God refers to God's possession, as well as His power to control. In Exodus 8–9, God declared that "the hand of the LORD" was at work in His plague upon the animals (NIV). In John 10:29 when Jesus declared "My Father . . . is greater than all; no one can snatch [My sheep] out of my Father's hand" (NIV), it is God's authority that is stated and assumed, but it is His possession that is being expressed.

David would pick up this picture of God and, possibly as no other writer could do, reflect upon his life in relationship to God in general, but in relationship to God's hand in particular. Just as Moses instructs the generation to tell the story of the mighty hand of God in the journey of His people, David writes his autobiography and often depicts it relative to the hand of God. David, perhaps like no other, teaches us that sin forces us under the controlling hand of God. In Psalm 32 we find David talking about what some theologians believe was a reference to his sin with Bathsheba. He said that when he kept silent about it, he suffered, because (among other things) God's hand was heavy upon him (Psalm 32:2–4). It is the image of someone trapping us to keep us from moving, and then pressing on us until we cry out, "Uncle!" (although, in David's case, *Father!* would have been more appropriate).

When we refuse to confess our sins before God, He will allow our sinful situation to hem us in and squeeze on us until we've had enough. Enough pain, enough heartache, enough loneliness, enough shallow living, enough joylessness, enough dry, parched wilderness. And then it's, "Father!"

In Psalm 32:4, David said his "moisture is turned into the drought of summer" (KJV). When we wander or walk away from the living water of God, He will let us get far enough out there, and then He will put His hand on us and *press*. He'll press long and hard enough on something that is dry until it eventually cracks and crumbles under the pressure. That's why, in his confession and repentance of his sin with Bathsheba in Psalm 51:8, David said, "Make me to hear joy and gladness; that the bones which thou hast broken may rejoice" (KJV). (Talk about pressure—God spiritually broke David's bones.)

Can you recall times or seasons in your life when it felt like you were living and walking in a dry desert? I'm talking about those times when nothing seemed to satisfy you. Those times when your life was just drifting—especially away from God.

There is another old song taken from the hymn book of the African American tradition that speaks of our inability to do anything without God: "Without Him I would fail. . . . Like a ship without a sail."[2]

David would say his life was adrift like a ship without a sail. He had sinned, but he had not confessed his sin. Isn't it interesting that we often foolishly assume that if we don't tell or confess our sins to God, He won't know? It's like we think, *I don't want God to know I did this, so I won't tell Him.* That's like a child who thinks that if he covers his eyes with his hands, nobody can see him.

What strikes me so significantly (and sometimes embarrassingly holds a mirror up to my own life) is that David talks about the hand of God and says how "day and night your hand was heavy on me" (Psalm 32:4 NIV). He is speaking of the time when he was in sin, when he wouldn't go to God and confess it. But God kept His hand on him. The weight of God's hand was "heavy" on David even when he had turned away from God in sin and brought about a sense of guilt. God held on to him to remind him not only that He was there, but that He was there in spite of what David had done.

In *Barnes' Notes*, Albert Barnes put it this way: "It was God who brought that guilt to his recollection; and God *kept* the recollection of it before his mind and on his heart and conscience so he could not throw it off."[3] This is a revelation of the truth that even in your sin, God does not abandon you, leave you, or forsake you. He will never kick you to the curb. He will not turn His back on you. He won't let you go, even when you let Him go.

Long ago when my son, Kendan, was learning to walk, I would wrap my hand around his and tell him, "Hold on to Daddy's hand." He would take a few steps and stumble. Then he would take a few more steps and start to fall. Every time he got excited about walking, he would let go of my hand and try to do it on his own. But when it looked like he was going down, I would simply tighten my grip on him. He let me go, but I never let go of him.

David let go of God's hand and ventured away from God on the path of sin, but when he reflected on his sinful season, he realized God's hand was still on him.

Have you ever let go of God's hand? I have been there, done that, got the T-shirt and the hat. So many times I have crossed the lines of the will and way of God. So many times I violated the Word of God, only to discover that He still had His hand on me. Like a fisherman who catches a fish and lets it splash and flail in the water, trying desperately to get away from its captor and release itself from the hook in its mouth, I (just like David) have swum in the waters of sin, turning away from the God of my salvation. However, the skilled fisherman gives the fish more and more line until the fish begins to tire. Then the catcher slowly reels him in, bringing him back to the boat. He never lets go. The fish gets tired, but the fisherman never gets fatigued; he waits, and then reels him in. God is the Catcher, the great Fisher of men.

A couple of years ago, my son Kendan and I were in the Bahamas on vacation and we decided to go deep-sea fishing. We had been out for several hours before we heard the long-awaited *click click click* of the reel, indicating Kendan had a bite on his line.

"This is a pretty good-sized one," the captain said as he helped Kendan get into a braced position. "This might take a while."

When they were solidly situated, the captain said, "Okay, now pull him in—just a little."

Kendan nodded and slowly tightened the slack a bit.

"Good. Now loosen the slack . . . play it out a little."

Kendan let off a bit. The fish drifted back a bit.

"Now, reel him in—just a tad."

After a few minutes of playing the fish in and out, it leapt out of the water, showing off its beautiful rainbow colors. After a few more minutes of repeatedly reeling it in, then letting it swim, reeling it in, letting it swim, I got it: the fish thought it was getting away when the slack was off, but each time Kendan would tighten the slack, the fish would end up a little closer to the boat.

I have Kendan's fish mounted on the wall of my office to this day. Every time I look at it, I think of the victorious day when my son pulled that fish into the boat. It reminds me of those times when I tried to run away, swim away, get away, "sin away" from God, only to discover that, as David had learned, His hand was still on me, lovingly reeling me back to Himself.

The hand of God is a hand of giving and provision and kindness. But it is also the hand of control: His hand can keep us from continuing in any direction that might destroy us.

The Deuteronomy 6 passage is not so much a revelation of what God did in previous generations, but a revelation of what He repeatedly does in *all* generations. Moses is reminding the people that God delivered them by His mighty hand, and they are to be on the lookout and know the mighty hand of God.

My rabbi friend says that if Deuteronomy 6 is the most important chapter in the Bible, then verse 4 is the most important verse in the Bible: "Hear, O Israel: The LORD our God, the LORD is one" (NIV). It begins with a declaration of who God the Blesser is, and a proclamation that all good things come from Him.

The word *Lord* is the word *Yahweh* or "Jehovah." It is the name God gave to Moses when Moses asked Him, "Who shall I say sent me?" (see Exodus 3:13). And God told Moses, in verse 14, "I Am That I Am . . . Thus shalt thou say unto the children of Israel, I Am hath sent me unto you" (KJV). This name speaks of the eternal "is-ness" of God. He is the God of the eternal now. He is the God who is eternally present. He is the God who am. He am *am*. He never was *was*. He never will be will *be*. He just . . . *am*. He am what He is, and He is what He am (that's bad English, but it's good theology).

## TALK ABOUT GOD

The Lord says you are to tell this to your children and your children's children; to your sons and to your daughters. The conduits through which revelation is to pass to the next generation are relationships. *Tell your sons and your son's sons.* It is stated in the context of a home that is consecrated to God. Thus, the home is meant to be the center of the revelation of God. The home is to be the divine schoolhouse, consecrated and committed to God.

The father is the teacher. The home is to be the center of truth. The home is where life makes up its mind. The home is to declare and display holiness. The home is to be the place for revelation, response, and responsibility. The curriculum is the Eternal God and how we are to live in relationship to Him.

How do we respond to the revelation of who God is? The answer is in Deuteronomy 6:5: "Love the LORD your God with all your heart and with all your soul and with all your strength" (NIV). Your response to God is to love Him and honor Him with your total being. With all of your mind, with all of your intellect, all of your decision-making capabilities, all of your will, all of your desires. Your response is to love Him.

Not only is there to be a response to this revelation of who God is, but our response also comes with a responsibility toward someone else: your children. "Thou shalt teach them diligently unto thy children, and shalt talk of them when thou sittest in thine house, and when thou walkest by the way, and when thou liest down, and when thou risest up. And thou shalt bind them for a sign upon thine hand, and they shall be as frontlets between thine eyes" (Deuteronomy 6:7–8 KJV).

This responsibility to God is personal. We are to love the Lord with all of our heart, mind, and soul. This love of God is to be demonstrated by depositing the Word of the Lord into the lives of our children by teaching them diligently.

Author Rabbi Samson Raphael Hirsch poetically expresses the priority of the Word of God like this:

> The Torah of God shall ever be to you like some ancient institution about which nobody takes much interest any more. Fresh like the light of dawn that greets you, fresh like the deep breath of pure air that you draw in is the Word of God to remain for you; every day given to you just "to-day," every day brought home afresh to you, and its contents to bring afresh to your mind the task of your life that new day. There is no greater enemy to our fulfilling the tasks of our lives than becoming blasé in carrying out, than loosing the freshness of recognizing them and enthusiasm in performing them.[4]

The instructions to "teach them [the words of God] diligently" are dramatically descriptive of how the Word is to be handled. The word used for *teach* is used only here. It means, "to sharpen." The Hebrew text says to "inoculate them sharply into thy son, and speak about them."[5] This edict contains two concepts: one refers to the manner and the other to the method of handling the words of God. It is the idea of sharpening as in sharpening a sword or arrow. It conjures an image of a hunter who wants to make sure his target will be well penetrated by the arrow directed to it. It emphasizes the intentions of the parent to ensure that the words of God are not dully or bluntly received, but that they penetrate the heart and soul of the child.

The Word also gives instructions on the method of imparting divine words. In the words of Rabbi Hirsch, it means:

> To teach something in short, sharp and easily remembered sentences . . . not just to say something or speak the words, but speak them, explain them . . . and if we take the two tasks together . . . then the instruction is given regarding the teaching of the Torah, first to imprint it in short, sharp, concise sentences and then impress it by conversing and debating on it.[6]

This is similar to teaching by the rabbinic method of what we might call an outline. First, the principle, the words, and the truth are stated; then it is expounded upon in more detail; then discussed and even debated, getting feedback and response from the learner. It is a picture of deliberate, diligent deposit of truth into the very being of the student, the learner, the child, and the next generation.

In Jewish culture, this process synthesizes the study of the Torah, the Mishna, and the Gemora. This three-part approach to Scripture involves concise sentences and more detailed embellishments into the nuances and depth of the teaching, followed by application and demonstration of clear understanding of that which was taught—without weak, wavering, or doubtful explanation. The Deuteronomy 6:7–8 passage suggests that you sharpen your words and the teaching, and then release them, aimed at the hearts of the hearers so that they might receive them into their very hearts and souls. The goal is that the student "gets it" and then incorporates what they have learned into the very fabric of their lives.

I once had a preaching professor in graduate school who taught us a teaching technique he called "blinking." Blinking meant you put forth a principle or truth, and then you would say it as many different ways as possible to help drive home the point of the passage. The idea is to do all you can to make sure they get it.

Deuteronomy 6:7 also says we are to *talk* about God's words and commandments when we sit and when we walk. Again, there is the idea of conversational instruction.

One commentary further elucidates Deuteronomy 6:7–8:

[B]y the expression "talk of them," Moses does not urge the people to empty talkativeness, to which many are too much inclined, but he would have them severally thus establish themselves and be teachers of each other. He enumerates these various engagements, lest that change of occupation by which the mind is wont to be distracted should withdraw the godly from the right path, as though he commanded them to make this their chief aim in whatever business they might be engaged.[7]

This "talking" is to be informal but intentional. It is said that as the disciples followed Jesus as their Rabbi, their Teacher, school was always in. They were always in class, whether beside a pool, on the side of a hill, or in a crowd of thousands, always taking spiritual notes as Jesus talked. In Luke 24:32 they even described a lesson from Jesus as giving them "heart burn": "Did not our heart burn within us, while he talked with us by the way, and while he opened to us the scriptures?" (KJV).

The goal of the Father is to touch the heart of His children with the fire of the Spirit and the spirit of the Word. The fact is, the disciples were always learning from Jesus; it was not just a part-time activity. For us, it is a call for parents (fathers in particular) to intentionally invest time in and with their children. Author G. H. Hall explains:

The covenant community had an obligation to pass on the covenant requirements to the next generation. Failure to do so jeopardized the people of God, and God's witness in the world faced extinction. Therefore, educating the children (literally "sons") was crucial. . . . In Proverbs "sons" means "pupils." . . . Although the evidence is scarce, it seems that education of the children in early Israel was the father's responsibility.[8]

This is the exhortation to strategically weave divine truth into the fabric of the everyday lives of our children. Some fathers have "date nights" with their kids. This investment of time is the most valuable investment both parents can make. From their early youthful days, children should be taught how to integrate the truth of the Lord into daily challenges, decisions, and choices. (As just one of many examples, the prevalence of bullying in our society might be short-circuited if the foundation of social interaction were based on the basic law of love found in the Word of God in Leviticus 19:18 and Matthew 22:39: "Love your neighbor as Yourself" [NIV]).

Even music can be used to talk about God. The word used in Deuteronomy 6:7 for *speaking* or *talking* is also used in Judges 5:12, where Deborah is said to sing a song. Many of us learned the ABCs through a little song. Books of the Bible and various scriptures are also adapted to music as a method of teaching.

In her blog post titled "Using Music as a Teaching Tool for Kids," Margarita Tartakovsky explains the use of music as an effective tool in teaching and learning:

> Music is a valuable teaching tool. It makes complex concepts more accessible and enjoyable. It facilitates language learning. Upbeat or uplifting music also may enhance cognitive abilities. Music appears to light up various regions of the brain related to language, hearing and motor control. . . . When listening to songs we tend to compare new images with past memories, which involves the association cortex . . . . "elements of musical surprise activate the cerebellum."[9]

## THE WALK OF GOD

The next phrase in Deuteronomy 6:7 that instructs us how to love God and follow His commands and ways is that we are to do so "when you walk along the road" (NIV). That is, how we comport ourselves in life, how we walk our path as followers of Christ.

One of the ministries at our church is called Rites of Passage, a program directed to the next generation of boys making the tricky and often challenging transition to men. It's a yearlong engagement of young boys and men who serve as tutors, overseers, and role models. It is a military model of drill sergeants, team building, and intentional teaching of biblical principles, both formally and informally, plus practical lessons on etiquette, respect for elders, and especially how to honor and esteem women.

Proverbs 27:17 says, "As iron sharpens iron, so one person sharpens another" (NIV). Yet, some of the boys in our group have never had a male figure as a role model. A few have never had direct contact with a man in their life. It was said once that during a Sunday school class when the lesson was to learn the Lord's Prayer, upon being taught the opening line, "Our Father in heaven," one of the children raised a hand and asked, "Teacher, what's a father?" If a young man never had a father to teach him how to walk properly down the precarious and jagged roads of life, how will he learn? As author M. Rutledge McCall put it in his book *Slipping into Darkness*, "A youngster will never have an opportunity to be a man if he's never treated like a man, with respect, dignity and honor. Likewise, if he is never shown these traits and qualities, he can never imitate them."[10]

The idea of one's walk speaks of their lifestyle. There is a sense in which "walk" is a summary of what has been talked. The way in which you "walk by the way" is more than picking up and putting down your feet; it's the idea of how you walk through life. Your presence in the marketplace, at work, out in the world, how you live before others, how you represent your relationship with the Lord after the benediction, after you close your hymn book, after you take off your choir robe, after you leave the morning worship or leave your small group gathering. That trait is an ability and a blessing that is handed down from one generation to the next.

## SUNUP TO SUNDOWN

At the end of Deuteronomy 6:7 we arrive at the instruction to teach when we lie down and when we rise up. Educating the next generation when you lie down and when you rise up implies the model of a prayer life. Prayer was part of the daily routine of the people of God; three times daily, four times on the Sabbath, and up to five times on Yom Kippur.

An Irish nun named Dr. Marie-Henry Keane, one of my scholastic mentors, helped shape my life at Oxford University and taught me an adage that has left an indelible imprint on my life. Dr. Keane said: "We should order our lives around the rhythms of our relationships with God." I am reminded of this most often when I think of the discipline of prayer.

I must say I have been impressed (and to a degree made ashamed) by the diligence of my Jewish friends, and even some Muslims, in their steadfast commitment to the times of daily prayer. I have been on airplanes where Jews would put on prayer cloths and Muslims would even take out a prayer rug and put it in the middle of the aisle of the plane at their assigned times of daily prayer. No hesitation. No self-consciousness. No shame. Many Jews and Muslims seem to drift into a sort of spirit zone and recite their prayers at a whisper. Never ostentatiously or in a manner to impress others or draw attention to themselves, but nonetheless faithful to the times of prayer. They had obviously ordered their lives around the rhythms of prayer. (Many Jewish families even have a mezuzah on the door frame of their homes, a visible indication that this is a house of prayer.)

We should allow our children to openly hear and see us pray—and not just for them, but also for the practical aspects of life. It is through our observable prayer life that our kids learn how God is involved in our daily existence. It is good for them to see the relationship between our prayers and the visible manifestations of God's hand in our lives.

In Psalm 139:2, the psalmist picks up the injunction of teaching when we rise up and when we lie down when he says to the Lord, "You know my sitting down and my rising up" (NKJV). May our children likewise know that our lying down and rising up is ordered by our relationship with the Lord.

## TALKING GOD IN PUBLIC

So far, we are instructed to pass on the blessing of our relationship within the confines of our personal, intimate relationship with our children in our home. However, as we continue with this great instructional manual of Deuteronomy 6, we go outside. We go public. Regarding how we live out our relationship with our Lord and the Word of our Lord, we are told in Deuteronomy 6:8 to "bind them as a sign on your hand, and they shall be as frontlets between your eyes" (NKJV).

These "frontlets," small headbands and armbands that you may have seen some Jewish men wear, are thin strips of leather attached to a small one-and-a-half-inch by one-and-a-half-inch box or case that contains scriptures representing one's loyalty and commitment to the Word of God. It is bound to their head so everything they think is under the authority of God. It is bound to their hand so everything they do is under the authority of God. They are bound or wrapped around the arm and meticulously positioned between the eyes, physically and metaphorically connecting the head, heart, and hand, as symbols of intellect, heart, and might. Spiritually, they represent the consistency between one's head, heart, and hand; what we think, what we feel, and what we do. It is a part of their lifestyle.

We are also "bound" to manifest the responsibility of educating our children and passing on the blessing of God. It is our whole life, our entire soul, our consuming passion. Our life should be bound up with this commitment. And it is to be passed to the next generation. Rabbi Hirsch writes:

> The acknowledgement of the "oneness" of God, the giving up of the whole of our lives and wishes to this One God with all our heart and all our soul and all our fortune which we are daily to bring to mind as being the whole of our life's task and the theme of our own education and of our educating our children, this we are to

bind on our hands as a symbol of "binding duty," and bind on our forehead as a symbol of "directing our eyes and thoughts."[11]

If you live in or near a Jewish neighborhood, you might have seen Jewish residents walking at certain times of the day. They will not ride bicycles or drive a vehicle, because it is a part of their consecration not to work on the Sabbath. When you see them walking, sometimes they have prayer shawls over them, which is in dedication to God. But these phylacteries also are used in their homes on the doorposts. It reminds them that whenever they go in or out, they go in honor of the Word of God that covers their comings and goings. It is an open demonstration of their consecration to the Lord and to His Word. It is personal, public, and parental. It establishes the priority of a godly home. The greatness of a nation is based on the godliness of the institution of family, of home, within that nation.

The secularism and humanism in our schools is moving society further and further away from biblical principles. As an academician, as a professor, and as a college president, I often say to students, "Make sure you take Jesus with you, because if you don't take Him with you, you probably won't find Him when you get there."

We are to teach our children, the next generation. The word *teach* speaks of deliberateness, as in a verb. You are the primary teacher of your child. Moses says we are to teach our children *diligently*. Deuteronomy 6:7 says there are things that you should do formally and informally in teaching our children. The mandate of this revelation to parents assumes *intent*. Your children will not learn by accident; they learn by observation, by talking, by intentional teaching, by experiential osmosis.

There's a particular kind of home that should be established when you live your life under the authority of the Word and will of God. The point Moses was making was that there should be something different about your home and your life that causes those inside and outside of the home to be intrigued by it. Deuteronomy 6:20 says there will come a time when "your children will ask" (NLT). A paraphrase of this might be the time *should* come when your children *should* ask, "Why do we pray in this house?" "Why do we say these words over a meal before we eat?" "Why do we read the Bible?" The day should come when the people who visit your home should ask, "Why did you stop us and say those words before we ate?" "Why do you do the things you do?" "Why do you live the way you live?"

In other words, the pattern of your life should provoke questions from your children and even from the casual or outside observer. Your life is to be a constant, living example of the mighty hand of God. The next generation should see that the previous generation is a demonstration and testimony of the power of God. The progression from the hearts of the parents to the hearts of the children should be marked by teaching points when lived out in public before the world that say, "God did this!" Because the time will come (and *should* come if you're striving to live your life God's way) when they will ask, "What does all of this mean?" That's the time when you should be able to point at some places and predicaments and experiences in your life and say, "Nobody but God alone made it all possible."

Everyone should have some *nobody but God* spots in their

life. The house you live in—*nobody but God* could have given you that. When you go from a bus pass to a car key—*nobody but God*. When you proudly watch that child walk across the stage at graduation—*nobody but God*. When you remember how hard it was to raise that child as a single mother or father and that child goes on to a life of success and productivity, *nobody but God*.

Your story is really about God's story. Tell people the story of God's love, God's provision, God's grace, God's mercy in your life. The best way to pass the blessing is to talk God talk and tell the story of God's presence and power in your life. So tell the story. If that's the only thing you pass to the next generation, then you will have done well, God's good and faithful servant.

The next generation is watching.

# ACKNOWLEDGMENTS

It is always interesting and challenging when you move into "thank you" mode. When my mind presses the rewind button, it appears to get stuck. I am but the product of amazing men and women who have spoken and sown into my life.

Over forty years ago, coming out of the fog of a relational failure, broken commitments, and falling down and rising again, the light in life was turned on by the Lord in the person of my high school friend and life partner, Togetta S. Ulmer. I am grateful to her parents, Willie and Hazel Tanner, for passing the baton of holiness, perseverance, and godliness to her. She and I have been "through many dangers, toils, and snares," and through it all we have learned to trust in Jesus, we have learned to trust in God. She is forever the light of my life, the beat of my heart, and the wind beneath my wings. She is my Kitten!

I thank my four beautiful children, RoShaun, Keniya, Kendan, and Jessica. There is nothing like being constantly aware that when I come out of pulpit, off the stage, and out of the spotlight of the world, you guys have seen me in my housecoat and house shoes, and you always remind me of the power of the love and grace of God. I pass it on to you. To Shiria, my one and only niece, goddaughter, adopted daughter who shares the Ulmer name and to whom I have tried to pass the generational blessings that have been passed to me. I love you all.

I am humbled and honored to have been blessed with grandchildren who are the recipients of the generational blessings invested in me. Kamryn, Ayari, Raegan, Aniya, Bailee, and Jonathan:

May you know the Father of your father's father. May you know that our God shall supply all your needs as you walk in righteousness before Him. You are gifts to me from a loving God. I realize that the bar has been set pretty high for you. But you can do and be anything you desire to be. I hope you know that Papa loves you, and you can do nothing in life to change that. I hope you pass on the tradition of annual family vacations. You can't imagine how much Papa loves you. I pass on to you this truth that my father passed to me: "Always shoot for the stars; there are stars beyond the moon. And if you miss, you will land in the atmosphere of a star." LOL! Don't worry—I didn't understand when my dad said it to me. One day you will.

To the men of our family: Jody, John, and Kendan. I remain amazed that God would allow me to father you. On the headstone of my father, George Ulmer, there is this phrase that he said over and over. He would especially say it after holidays, special occasions, and the ups and downs of being a father. In fact, I unknowingly overheard him say to my mother, Ruth, "Well, Bae, I DID MY BEST" . . . I pass this baton to you. Always try to land at a place where you can say, "I DID MY BEST!"

Thank you to my only sister and brother, Kathy and Douglas. From growing up and playing together at 1124 Tudor, E. St. Louis, to having the honor of being your pastor, thank you for standing with me even during those seasons when it seemed that our lives were taking separate paths. You have always been there. I love you dearly.

To my assistant for more years than I can remember, Ivory Beasley. Thank you for keeping my life on track in spite of sticking with me through the crazy times. Thank you to the pastoral staff of the Family of Champions. Steven Johnson, Gail Dvorak, George Thompson, Kasey Whitney, Lucious Hicks, J. P. Foster, Trevon Evans, Sonya Byous, Bob Gay, and Omar Muhammad, we have seen the unchanging faithfulness of God in the changing times of ministry. You are true champions.

To my friend, mentor, life coach, Dr. Sam Chand. I make my living talking, and I am quite frustrated when I cannot express the depth of gratitude I owe you for being in my life over the past twenty years. Thank you, my friend.

To my spiritual father, Larry Titus. You have inspired the essence of this book as I have seen and experienced the incarnation of the principle of passing blessings to the next generation. I am in awe of how you have subdivided yourself around the world to hundreds of men and can't image how you know all of our names and treat us as if we were your only (spiritually) begotten sons!

To my writing partner, editor, agent, and precious friend, Michael McCall. We have been through the jungles of the publishing world and come out holding each other's hands, pressing on to the next project, and thanking God for each other. Thank you for being my brother.

To Ted Squires, who hooked me up with Worthy Publishing. And, finally, to the amazing Worthy team: Byron Williamson, CEO and publisher; Jeana Ledbetter, vice president and associate publisher; Leeanna Nelson, managing editor and author relations; Cat Hoort, marketing and publicity director; Bart Dawson, interior design manager; and Kyle Olund, executive editor. Thank you for partnering with me on this project. I pray you never have another client that bugs you as much as I did. You have been a joy to work with. LET'S DO IT AGAIN!

# NOTES

## Chapter 1

1  "My Shot" lyrics by Lin-Manuel Miranda, from the Original Broadway Cast Recording of the stage play *Hamilton*, Genius, https://genius.com/Lin-manuel-miranda-my-shot-lyrics#.

2  Since 1973, when the Supreme Court handed down its decision in *Roe v. Wade*, there have reportedly been well over 54 million abortions. Some estimates put the number as high as 60 million between 1973 and 2014, based on figures reported by the Guttmacher Institute, a sexual and reproductive health research and policy organization. As of March 18, 2012, Guttmacher tracked roughly 49.3 million abortions through 2008, with projections of 926,190 for 2015–2017. (Guttmacher has estimated possible undercounts of 3–5 percent, thus, an additional 3 percent is factored into their overall total); "United States Abortion," Guttmacher Institute, https://www.guttmacher.org/united-states/abortion.

## Chapter 2

1  Leonard Sweet, *Giving Blood: A Fresh Paradigm for Preaching* (Grand Rapids: Zondervan, 2014), 38.

2  Wikipedia, s.v. "United States at the 2008 Summer Olympics," last modified March 1, 2018, 18:09, https://en.wikipedia.org/wiki/United_States_at_the_2008_Summer_Olympics#Medalists.

3  Wikipedia, s.v. "United States at the 2005 Summer Olympics," last modified May 27, 2018, 10:40, https://en.wikipedia.org/wiki/United_States_at_the_2004_Summer_Olympics#Medalists.

4  Sam Borden, "For U.S. Relayers, Dread of Another Dropped Baton," *New York Times* online, July 23, 2012, http://www.nytimes.com/2012/07/23/sports/olympics/olympics-2012-us-track-relays-hope-to-avoid-another-baton-drop.html.

5  Rudyard Kipling, *Rewards and Fairies*, from a chapter titled "Brother Square Toes" (New York: Doubleday, Page, 1910).

6  *PBS NewsHour*, "Harry Belafonte: To Realize Martin Luther King Jr.'s Dream, White America Needs to Change Course," April 6, 2018, PBS, 7:36, https://www.google.com/amp/s/www.pbs.org/newshour/amp/show/harry-belafonte-to-realize-martin-luther-king-jr-s-dream-white-america-needs-to-change-course.

## Chapter 3

1  Jentzen Franklin, story of the Maypure tribe told at the 2016 gathering of Empowered21 in Jerusalem.

2  Sarah Griffiths, "How Will We Speak in 100 Years? 90% of Languages Will Become Extinct Because of Migration, Linguist Claims," *Daily Mail*, January 20, 2015, http://

www.dailymail.co.uk/sciencetech/article-2910238/How-speak-100-years-90
-languages-extinct-migration-linguist-claims.html.

3   Raveena Aulakh, "Dying Languages: Scientists Fret as One Disappears Every 14 Days,"
    *Toronto Star*, April 15, 2013, https://www.thestar.com/news/world/2013/04/15
    /dying_languages_scientists_fret_as_one_disappears_every_14_days.html.

4   Treatment for Alcohol Abuse & Drug Abuse Memphis, TN, "Compulsive Texting,"
    *Intensive Outpatient Program* (blog), Mental Health Resources, October 13, 2012, http://
    www.alcoholismdrugabuse.com/compulsive-texting/.

## Chapter 4

1   "The Proof Is In: Father Absence Harms Children," National Fatherhood Initiative,
    https://www.fatherhood.org/father-absence-statistic.

2   Luke Rosiak, "Fathers Disappear from Households across America," *Washington Times*,
    December 25, 2012, https://www.washingtontimes.com/news/2012/dec/25
    /fathers-disappear-from-households-across-america/.

3   Kim Parker and Gretchen Livingston, "7 Facts About American Dads," Fact Tank, Pew
    Research Center, last modified June 13, 2018, http://www.pewresearch.org/fact-tank
    /2018/06/13/fathers-day-facts/.

4   Parker and Livingston.

5   Parker and Livingston.

6   M. Rutledge McCall, *Slipping into Darkness: A True Story from the American Ghetto*
    (2000; repr. Archangel House, 2002), 379.

## Chapter 5

1   Danniebelle Hall, "Danniebelle Hall—Ordinary People Lyrics," SongLyrics, http://www
    .songlyrics.com/danniebelle-hall/ordinary-people-lyrics/.

2   Booker T. Washington, "Booker T. Washington Quote," iz Quotes, http://izquotes.com
    /quote/276773.

## Chapter 6

1   Marvin Gaye, "Make Me Wanna Holler," Inner City Blues, 1971.

2   Rin Hamburgh, "The Lost Art of Handwriting," *Guardian*, August 21, 2013, US
    edition, https://www.theguardian.com/lifeandstyle/2013/aug/21/lost-art-handwriting.

3   Michael Lipka, "A Closer Look at America's Rapidly Growing Religious 'nones,'" Fact
    Tank, Pew Research Center, May 13, 2015, http://www.pewresearch.org/fact-tank
    /2015/05/13/a-closer-look-at-americas-rapidly-growing-religious-nones/.

4   Lipka.

## Chapter 7

1   PC Study Bible, *McClintock and Strong Cyclopedia* (Biblesoft, Inc., 2001, 2003, 2005,
    2006).

2   Kenneth Ulmer, *In His Image* (New Kensington, PA: Whitaker House, 2005).

3   Donald Lawrence, "Encourage Yourself," Donald Lawrence Lyrics, AZLyrics.com, https://www.azlyrics.com/lyrics/donaldlawrence/encourageyourself.html.

## Chapter 8

1   Charles Baudelaire, "The Generous Gambler," https://genius.com/Charles-baudelaire -the-generous-gambler-annotated and https://lagazettedesydney.wordpress.com/2015 /05/02/a-very-actual-old-french-poem-the-generous-gambler/.

2   Tony Evans, *Raising Kingdom Kids: Giving Your Child a Living Faith* (Colorado Springs: Focus on the Family, 2014), 10.

3   BibleStudy.org, "Levels of Heaven?" The Bible Study Site, http://www.biblestudy.org /question/are-there-different-levels-of-heaven.html.

4   Tony Evans, "Tony Evans Speaks on Having Victory in Spiritual Warfare," Tony Evans: The Urban Ulternative (website), Victory in Spiritual Warfare page, https://tonyevans .org/tony-evans-victory-in-spiritual-warfare/.

5   Ray C. Stedman, *Spiritual Warfare: Winning the Daily Battle with Satan* (Portland: Multnomah Press, 1975), 47.

6   Stedman, 48–49.

7   Stedman, 56.

8   Prepare to roll on the floor laughing when watching the 1998 Chris Tucker and Jackie Chan movie *Rush Hour*. The serious message of the song "War" takes on a comedic flare in the movie when Jackie Chan tries to mimic Chris Tucker singing the song to the thumping radio beat in Tucker's convertible sports car. Chan's rhythmically spastic version will bring laughter, chuckles, and smiles over the hook line, "War—*HUH!* What is it good for? Absolutely *nothin'!*" *Rush Hour*, directed by Brett Ratner, featuring Jackie Chan and Chris Tucker (Burbank, CA: New Line Cinema: Roger Birnbaum Productions, 1998).

9   Fritz Rienecker, *A Linguistic Key to the Greek New Testament* (Grand Rapids, MI: Zondervan, 1980), 485.

10  Ruth Paxson, *The Wealth Walk and Warfare of the Christian* (Old Tappan, NJ: Fleming H. Revell, 1939), 214.

11  Evans, *Raising Kingdom Kids,* 13–14.

12  Evans, 14.

13  Evans, 14.

## Chapter 10

1   Fantastic Four, "The Whole World Is a Stage," Lyrics, LyricsFreak, http://www.lyricsfreak .com/f/fantastic+four/the+whole+world+is+a+stage_20846316.html.

2   William Shakespeare, "All the World's a Stage," *As You Like It*, act 2, scene 7, Poetry Foundation, https://www.poetryfoundation.org/poems/56966/speech-all-the-worlds -a-stage.

3   7 Cultural Mountains, http://www.7culturalmountains.org/.

4   Leland Ryken, James C. Wilhoit, and Tremper Longman III, eds., *Dictionary of Biblical Imagery* (Downers Grove, IL: InterVarsity, 1998).

5   Ryken, Wilhoit, and Longman III.

6   Ryken, Wilhoit, and Longman III.

7   Leonard Sweet and Frank Viola, *Jesus: A Theography* (Nashville: Thomas Nelson, 2012). Kindle.

8   Albert Barnes, *Barnes' Notes*, PC Study Bible (Biblesoft, Inc., 2003, 2005, 2006, 2007).

9   John F. Walvoord and Roy B. Zuck, eds., *Bible Knowledge Commentary/Old Testament*, Bible Knowledge (Colorado Springs, CO: Cook Communications Ministries, 2000).

10  PC Study Bible, *The Pulpit Commentary* (Biblesoft, Inc., 2001, 2003, 2005, 2006).

11  *Ben-Hur*, directed by William Wyler, featuring Charlton Heston (Los Angeles: Metro-Goldwyn-Mayer, 1959).

12  Spiros Zodhiates, ed., *The Complete Word Study Dictionary: New Testament*, World Study, rev. ed. (Chattanooga, TN: AMG International, Inc., 1993).

**Chapter 11**

1   *Magnum Force* (sequel to the movie *Dirty Harry*), directed by Ted Post, featuring Clint Eastwood (Burbank, CA: The Malpaso Company and Warner Bros., 1973).

2   Warren Baker and Eugene Carpenter, eds. *The Complete Word Study Dictionary: Old Testament*, World Study (Chattanooga, TN: AMG Publishers, 2003).

3   Henri Nouwen, *The Wounded Healer* (New York: Image Books, 1979).

4   Carl E. Pickhardt, "Adolescence and the Influence of Parents," *Psychology Today*, October 18, 2010, https://www.psychologytoday.com/blog/surviving-your-childs-adolescence/201010/adolescence-and-the-influence-parents.

5   Pickhardt.

6   CBN.com, "A Parent's Influence," The Christian Broadcasting Network, Inc., http://www1.cbn.com/family/a-parent%27s-influence.

7   CBN.com.

8   Baker and Carpenter, *The Complete Word Study Dictionary*.

**Chapter 12**

1   Ulmer, *In His Image*.

2   Beatrice Brown, "Without God I Could Do Nothing," *The New National Baptist Hymnal* (Nashville: National Baptist Publishing Board, 1959), 320.

3   Barnes, *Barnes' Notes*.

4   Rabbi Samson Raphael Hirsch, *The Pentateuch*, vol. 5 (Gateshead: Judaica Press, 1989), 97–98.

5   Hirsch, 98.

6   Hirsch, 98–99.

7   PC Study Bible, *Calvin's Commentaries* (Biblesoft, Inc., 2005–2006).

8   G. H. Hall, *Deuteronomy* (Joplin, MO: College Press, 2000) 139–40.

9   Margarita Tartakovsky, "Using Music as a Teaching Tool for Kids," *World of Psychology* (blog), Psych Central, https://psychcentral.com/blog/archives/2013/09/19/using-music-as-a-teaching-tool-for-kids/.

10  McCall, *Slipping into Darkness*.

11  Hirsch, *The Pentateuch*, 103.

# ABOUT THE AUTHOR

**KENNETH C. ULMER** is senior pastor of Faithful Central Bible Church in Southern California.

Dr. Ulmer participated in the study of ecumenical liturgy and worship at Magdalen College at Oxford University in England. He has served as an instructor in pastoral ministry and homiletics at Grace Theological Seminary, as an instructor of African-American preaching at Fuller Theological Seminary in Pasadena, as an adjunct professor at Biola University (where he served on the board of trustees), and as an adjunct professor at Pepperdine University. He is past president of The King's University, Dallas, Texas, founded by Dr. Jack Hayford; he is also a founding board member and currently an adjunct professor at The King's. For over two decades he has served as director of The King's at Oxford (a summer session of The King's University held at Oxford University, United Kingdom). He has served as mentor in the doctor of ministry degree programs at United Theological Seminary and presently at Payne Theological Seminary.

Dr. Ulmer received his bachelor of arts degree in broadcasting and music from the University of Illinois. After accepting his call to the ministry, Dr. Ulmer was ordained at Mount Moriah Missionary Baptist Church in Los Angeles, and shortly afterward founded Macedonia Bible Baptist Church in San Pedro, California. He has studied at Pepperdine University, Hebrew

Union College, the University of Judaism, Christ Church, and Magdalen College at Oxford University in England. He received a PhD from Grace Graduate School of Theology in Long Beach, California (later to become the West Coast Campus of Grace Theological Seminary). He received his doctor of ministry from United Theological Seminary, and was awarded an honorary doctor of divinity from Southern California School of Ministry.

In 1994, Dr. Ulmer was consecrated bishop of Christian education and founding member of the Bishops Council of the Full Gospel Baptist Church Fellowship. He's a life member of the board of directors of the Gospel Music Workshop of America. Dr. Ulmer is the presiding bishop over the Macedonia International Bible Fellowship, with churches representing South Africa, Great Britain, and the US. He serves as co-chair of Global Leaders Network, and co-chair of Empowered 21, an organization that is helping shape the future of the Spirit-empowered movement throughout the world by focusing on crucial issues facing the movement and connecting generations for intergenerational blessing and impartation.

Dr. Ulmer has written several books, including *A New Thing* (a reflection on the Full Gospel Baptist Movement); *Spiritually Fit to Run the Race* (a guide to godly living); *In His Image: An Intimate Reflection of God* (an update of his book *The Anatomy of God*); *Making Your Money Count: Why We Have It—How to Manage It; Knowing God's Voice;* and *Passionate God.*

Dr. Ulmer and his wife are residents of Los Angeles, California, and have been married for thirty-six years. They have three daughters, one son, and six grandchildren.

## IF YOU ENJOYED THIS BOOK, WILL YOU CONSIDER SHARING THE MESSAGE WITH OTHERS?

Mention the book in a blog post or through Facebook, Twitter, Pinterest, or upload a picture through Instagram.

Recommend this book to those in your small group, book club, workplace, and classes.

Head over to facebook.com/drkennethculmer, "LIKE" the page, and post a comment as to what you enjoyed the most.

Tweet "I recommend reading #generationblessing by @BishopUlmer // @worthypub"

Pick up a copy for someone you know who would be challenged and encouraged by this message.

Write a book review online.

**Visit us at worthypublishing.com**

twitter.com/worthypub

instagram.com/worthypub

facebook.com/worthypublishing

youtube.com/worthypublishing